THE WAY OF SILENT LOVE

In the One

neither Master nor disciple
is greater

for both are god.

Evagrius Ponticus

Contents

Contents

Acknowledgement

The Translator gratefully acknowledges the assistance of
a Sister of the Community of St Clare
who checked the translation against the French original
and whose invaluable suggestions
almost invariably have been incorporated.

Translator's Note

Most of the treasures that have come to us through the ages from Carthusian Charterhouses were never meant for publication, and these novice conferences on the Beatitudes, given as part of the formation programme between 1975 and 1990, are no exception. The author notes that they are 'highly personal' and that, in the tradition of the desert fathers, many quotations were included from memory; thus it has not been possible to trace every reference.

Mention of the desert fathers is not a mere pious gesture. The present author hands on this tradition newly minted. There is a sense in which his text cannot be read 'literally' enough, not in the constricting sense of fundamentalism or at the level of linear and chronological biography, but rather as a key that opens a door into the vast love of Christ.

For he understands that obedience is not about arbitrary exercise of and blind submission to power, but rather the longing of kenosis calling to kenosis, the self-emptying of the spiritual parent awakening a similar longing in the novice, because this self-emptying is not only the creative movement of divine life, but the capacity for a welcoming spaciousness in which Christ comes to dwell.

The first conference is fundamental to the whole. In it the author speaks of the tradition of the spiritual parent who can 'support, affirm, give a certain visible and concrete reality to the teaching and action of the Master within. He can remove . . . the more or less hidden obstacles to that action.' The spiritual parent does this 'not so much by his teaching, nor even by his example . . . but rather by prayer. The father, in the image of Christ, must take upon himself the trials, the imperfections and even the sins of those he guides; he must expiate them and hold them before God in prayer. In a word, the Father Master is worth what his love is worth.'

To put this another way, the poverty of the spiritual parent creates a space in which not only Christ may dwell but in which the novice may dwell in Christ. The prayer of the spiritual parent, male or female, is the womb in which the novice begins new life as an embryo.

The first and most fundamental exchange is the relinquishing to the spiritual parent by the novice of pain, fears, sins and struggles so that the second birth may occur, of which Christ speaks to Nicodemus. Until these obstacles, the struggles with illusion of the illusory self, are relinquished, until stillness, poverty-purity-peace are established in the opened heart, new life cannot be gestated, and the novice cannot know the true freedom in Christ which 'must finally enable the novice to be independent of the person who formed him'.

This requires immense poverty, letting-be, on the part of the spiritual parent in order that the novice-embryo may be soaked in the love of the indwelling Christ. New life depends on the humbly audacious knowledge that 'everything, absolutely everything, depends on Christ, is gratuitously given from his love. Christ is able to do everything', a knowledge that is not 'an abstract truth . . . but rather . . . the reality that I am in the deepest part of myself in Christ, or rather, Christ in me'.

A divine exchange takes place in this womb of prayer as the novice relinquishes obstacles and hindrances and is infused with new life. Christ is born in the novice even as the novice is born into the kingdom of Christ, giving birth to Christ in the Father's heart, to will with Christ, in joy, in peace and love, God's eternity in each moment.

In an age when we have spent decades gazing helplessly at the dead child of religious metaphor, these conferences restore it to us, living, washed with the tears of repentance and the joy of the vision of God. It has been a great privilege to be entrusted with their translation; more, it has been a life-changing task, undertaken with awe and with joy. So may they be for those who delight in reading them.

Feast of the Epiphany, 1993

CONFERENCE I

It might have been more satisfactory to be able to present you with a complete formation programme, the principles on which it is based, my own personal preferences, etc.

But I will spare you all of that; firstly, because that would have been very difficult to effect, even for one who had exercised the charge of Father Master for many years; almost impossible for someone like myself who takes it up for the first time. Secondly, because it might have given a false impression of monastic formation.

Monastic formation is not a question of a body of doctrine which the novice is to learn. It is the transmission of a life – incarnate life, because we have a share in humanity; incarnate life, therefore, body and soul. The body manifests the practical expression of the way members of a group live together and the rules and customs that govern their common life. The soul is the ideal towards which they strive, the interior spirit which carries them onward; the love that gives life to their outward observance, that quality that lies beyond definition: the spirit that gives them life; the spirit which has its source in the self-outpouring of God, because it is their response to a particular call of God that is continually kindled at this divine flame – otherwise there would be a corpse, not a body. The outward body of our life makes no sense without regard to a reality that surpasses the human sphere and all created reality: the self-communication of divine life that the Father gives us through Christ by the working of his Spirit.

At its heart, the wellspring of our Carthusian life is divine love, and the goal of our lives is divine love; and the way into which formation seeks to move us can be nothing other than divine love, that is to say, the love of God poured out in our hearts by the Holy Spirit who dwells in us (Romans 5:5). The Spirit alone can search the depths of God, the Spirit alone communicates the life and love of God, the Spirit alone, the anointing that teaches us from within, is able to guide us in the ways of God, unto the Father.

For the solitary whose gaze seeks God alone beyond all that is created, the ultimate guide can only be the divine Master who dwells in the heart. So then, what use is a Father Master? Not very much if one sees in him only a man with certain qualities, a particular experience, prudence, and a specific monastic polish. Of course he can transmit an abundance of useful information at a certain level; he can ground the outward person in a certain discipline that allows insertion into the monastic milieu without too many hard knocks; he can mould a certain moral and ascetical perfection – but he cannot bestow God, he cannot enable entry into the intimacy of divine life. He is not able to do this for himself by means of his own resources and his own wisdom.

But as an instrument of God, if God wishes to use him, he can support, affirm, give a certain visible and concrete reality to the teaching and action of the Master within. He can remove in ourselves the more or less hidden obstacles to that action. We are so clumsy, so deaf, so blind because of our passions and egotism that we easily deceive ourselves in regard to what the Spirit wishes to say to us. We need to have it confirmed by a voice other than our own. And in the end, God, who knows our weakness, has adapted the economy of his salvation to our condition. This is the principle of incarnation.

The love of God is incarnate in Christ; the Spirit given to us is the Spirit of Christ. The light in our hearts finds its perfect reflection in the face of Christ, and through contemplation we are transfigured into his image.

> For it is the God who said, 'Let light shine out of darkness,' who has shone in our hearts to give the light of the knowledge of the glory of God in the face of Christ. (2 Corinthians 4:6)

> And we all, with unveiled face, beholding and reflecting the glory of the Lord, are being changed into his likeness from

one degree of glory to another; for this comes from the Lord who is the Spirit. (2 Corinthians 3:18)

I will not pause to extract the full richness of doctrine contained in these texts (see Feuillet, *Divine Wisdom in the Pauline Writings*). For our purposes it is enough to note here that the interior light of the Spirit corresponds to an incarnate light in, and reflected through, Christ; the one completes the other, each is unfulfilled without the other.

Christ continues in our own day, through his body, the Church, to communicate this outward light; through her, Christ sanctifies, guides and teaches us. He does this through sacraments, dogmas, teaching, etc., but also through human beings, through all who participate in the power of the Church, and to whom the Church, and therefore Christ, delegates his authority and his grace. It is to them he says, 'Whoever listens to you listens to me' (Luke 10:16).

By virtue of his office[1] the Father Master participates in the authority of the Church; he is the hand and the voice of Christ for the task entrusted to him, that is to say, novice formation. According to the Statutes, his role is to teach the observances of the Order, to mould the novice's behaviour, to guide him in the practice of the spiritual life, and to give him appropriate help in times of trial.

Obviously he is not infallible, no more than the Church, in each of his deeds. But he has a grace of office, and according to the measure of his docility, of his transparency, Christ speaks and acts in him. This demands a great receptivity to the light of the Spirit, divesting himself of his own lights and interests. He must therefore be a man of prayer. His role is that of John the Baptist, 'to go before the Lord in his sight to prepare his way, to give his people knowledge of salvation' (Luke 1:76–7). He is the friend whose joy is complete when the union of the bride and bridegroom is effected. And then he must efface himself: 'He must increase; I must decrease' (John 3:29–30).

Life is communicated more by contact, by infection, than by teaching; before teaching, one must be. But according to the Eastern tradition, it is not so much by his teaching, nor even by his example that the spiritual father helps his children, but rather by his prayer. The father, in the image of Christ, must take upon himself the trials, the imperfections and even the sins of those he guides; he must expiate them and hold them before God in prayer. In a word, the Father Master is worth what his love is worth.

For the novice's part, before anything else, let him regard his Father Master with the eyes of faith. Let him not stop because of his weaknesses, let him listen only to the voice of Christ, let him pay attention only to the hands of Christ, who is kneading him into shape. This is very important: this is the source of great peace, because what is happening is that the novice is learning to rely on God through the one he sends, and God will not allow the novice to be damaged; he knows how to draw benefit from the very unskilfulness and limitations of the one who is his instrument.

But we have seen that God does not work through the Father Master only on the outside; the Holy Spirit also guides from within. These two ways of working are divinely interwoven and complement each other in a wondrous harmony; it is always the same Spirit. The outward authority sets in motion the general principles which are applied individually with each novice. The Spirit's interior action marks the way completely differently for each person, for God wills each person to walk a unique and individual path. The Father Master ought, therefore, to be at the bidding of the Spirit, not listening solely to himself, but even more to the soul of the novice. His discernment should follow the coordinates traced by the Spirit in his heart. Certainly he needs to be extremely open and highly flexible; he should not be rigid about any idea or preconceived system, because the ways of God are not our ways. He should not seek to have the novice follow his own way, because each is different, each has his true hidden name, and each his own journey. The Father Master must have infinite respect for the creative word that God speaks in the soul of the novice and that reveals to him and creates in him his own deepest truth. In a word, the Father Master must have infinite respect for the person that is the novice, and consequently for his liberty and his responsibility: freedom which he will seek to make steadfast and self-aware; a sense of personal responsibility which he will try to awaken and sustain. It is evident that he cannot fulfil his role unless the novice in complete simplicity and candour reveals the impulses of grace in his soul, his difficulties and desires, etc. Thus, one of the most important aspects of his formation, with the assistance of the Father Master, is to learn how to discern which spirit is moving his heart. Throughout monastic tradition, it is primarily through the manifestations of 'thoughts' to his spiritual father that the novice learns how to do this. He must never hide his secret thoughts, in the largest sense, that is to say, all the positive or negative stirrings of his heart. 'But he who does what is true comes to the light, that it may be clearly seen that his deeds have been wrought in God' (John 3:21). It is essential that by the end of the novitiate the novice knows how to make the discernment of spirits for himself. He is going to live in solitude. He will be able to consult a more experienced father, especially in more difficult and important instances, but in the end the accountability for his acts is his own and, for the most part, he must know how to discern the spirits for himself. The formation of the novitiate, like all forms of education, must finally enable the novice to be independent of the person who formed him.

We can see clearly, then, that monastic formation cannot be realized without a trusting and open dialogue between the Father Master and the novice. Together they come to live in docility to the action of the Holy Spirit, by or through which Christ, the sole Master in truth, wishes to effect his design for holiness in the individual soul. This action is often hidden, baffling, subtle, and of extraordinary delicacy. This voice cannot be perceived without a spirit of humility and profound recollection. This is by way of speaking of the absolute necessity of prayer, true prayer. It is therefore imperative that we all pray one for another in order that the divine light may not be dimmed in us and among us, so that we do not fail this spirit of divine sensitivity, necessarily given for the realization of such a delicate and important work.

These few remarks should give you some idea of the spirit

in which I undertake my charge, difficult in all its aspects, which Christ has entrusted to me. The only reason that I am not daunted by the responsibility inherent in this office, the only reason that I am able to be peaceful about it, is that I know that of myself I am able to do absolutely nothing. Everything, absolutely everything, depends on Christ, is given gratuitously from his love. Christ is able to do everything. I know this, not as an abstract truth, outside of myself, but rather as the reality that I am in the deepest part of myself in Christ, or rather, Christ in me. This awareness that I have is one of the most precious fruits of life from my fourteen years in solitude.

You see, I am not burdening myself with a programme of detailed action or numerous principles. In the end, it is neither you nor I who leads the dance, it is God; you and I do not need to know the way in advance, we only need to entrust ourselves to the love of Christ, to the action of his Spirit. In this we will be led by a hidden path in the shadow of the cross, and in the radiance of the mystery of life of which it is the end, the eternal mystery of the Father.

1. Canon 561.1, Statutes 1. 9. 4.

to be consciously felt (as occasionally happens in divine contemplation); we cannot link it to a specific feeling (and feeling has no relation to the intensity of divine activity). Alone, the action of the Spirit can bestow purity of heart, 'that eye, by whose serene gaze the Spouse is wounded with love; that eye, pure and clean, by which God is seen.'[1]

This illustrates the importance of our extreme docility to the Holy Spirit. We, who pass the greatest part of our life in solitude and silence, need always to be attentive to the Word of God, free from all ties and ready to take wing to the Father at the first breath of the Spirit.

Purity of heart silences our unruly passions, our clouded egoism. Humility is born from the truth of ourselves, which we contemplate in the mirror of the Word of God. It is humility that does not give rise to despair but to hope, hope that confides everything in God, not resenting but loving the One who gives us all, the humility that gives us himself. Humility disposes us to receive his gifts, his fortitude, his inspirations, a participation in his knowledge and his love.

From a practical point of view, the monastic tradition teaches us the necessity of watchfulness over the heart so that it may become pure.

Exterior watchfulness: to flee occasions of evil, to withdraw from anxiety and preoccupation with the concerns of the world as far as possible (without neglecting the obligations of our life).

Interior watchfulness: we must watch our thoughts, our affections, all that comes from the heart, that is to say, in the depths of human life.

This is the vigilance, the *nepsis* of monastic tradition. 'You must watch the door of your heart continually and ask each suggestion: "Are you for us or against us?".'* We know from experience that we are frequently unable to discern the wolf from the lamb – the devil can clothe himself as an angel of light. This is the reason it is necessary to have a guide.[2]

This vigilance is never neurotic, it is not struck in self-analysis

* *Dictionnaire de Spiritualité* 3 c. 1036

without end. It is rather a considered and attentive observation that looks carefully at everything, and notes what remains ambiguous, so as to question it at the appropriate moment. All is peacefully done, without long interior dialogues, by means of a simple and intuitive judgement, that is more a question of an instinct for the good than analysis. The heart that is good spontaneously rejects what is questionable or, at least, feels uneasy about it.

At the same time, there can be highly complex cases, in which something which will be harmful in the long term can present itself under an attractive guise and apparent good. It is for this reason that we are counselled from the outset to submit all our thoughts to the spiritual father, because if it is given to us to make the initial choices as to what is good and what is bad, we may very well deceive ourselves at the beginning.

Among the movements of the heart and our thoughts, it is proper to distinguish between those that only touch the surface and disappear (better not to pay attention at all to these), and those that return with a certain insistence or with an emotional charge. These indicate a deep-seated propensity in the heart, a repressed desire (and therefore powerful), something uninte-grated; and it is in everyone's interest to manifest these recur-ring thoughts to the spiritual father so that he may apply the appropriate remedy. This spirit of vigilance is deeply embedded in monastic tradition. You know the Gospel for the feast of St Bruno: Luke 12:35–40.

> 'Let your loins be girded
> and your lamps burning,
> and be like men who are waiting for their master
> to come home from the marriage feast,
> so they can open to him at once when he comes and knocks.
> Blessed are those servants whom the master
> finds awake when he comes;
> truly, I say to you,
> he will gird himself and have them sit at table,
> and he will come and serve them.'

The vigil of Matins follows the same line of reasoning. In waiting for the Lord's coming, in watching for his visitation in our hearts, we become watchmen at the doors of our hearts and on the walls of the Church, so as not to be caught unawares by the forces of darkness, and to open to the Lord. For we do not keep vigil for ourselves alone, but for the whole Church, the light of our faith steadfast against the darkness. We have to be the vigilant heart of the Church.

Perhaps a better way to consolidate this vigilance and this discernment is to cultivate a sense of the presence of God, that is to say, not to preoccupy ourselves at first sight with the endless sequence of impressions and thoughts that pass before our mind and imagination, but positively to turn our gaze towards God, calmly, without tension or excessive stress. Everything in our life helps us: the liturgy, *lectio divina*, the word of God from which so many of our readings are woven, the deliberate absence of secular interests and desires, detachment from all that does not lead us to God.

In addition, at a practical and ordinary level, but realistically and effectively, the monastic tradition teaches the use of short prayers, ejaculations, whose repetition does not require a lot of intellectual effort, but is enough, during the tasks of the day, to nourish the flame of our love and to keep our heart turned towards God. Thus in the chapter on the 'occupations in cell' one reads: 'Indeed, we are exhorted to have constant recourse during work to short and, as it were, ejaculatory prayers.' This practice, and physical activity that does not require all our attention, permits us to linger in the presence of God. Furthermore, the Statutes continue: 'It sometimes happens also that the very weight of our work acts as a sort of anchor to the ebb and flow of our thought, thus enabling our heart to remain fixed on God without mental fatigue.'[3]

Further on,[4] the Statutes speak of the liberty of spirit that the monk ought to preserve in relation to his work in the cell. 'For it is fitting that the solitary, whose attention is fixed not so much on the work itself as on the goal he is aiming at, should at all times be able to keep his heart watchful.' (Note the relation between the notions of 'attention' and 'heart': it is evident that 'heart' is meant to be understood in the biblical sense.)

In this way, it is possible to work without leaving habitual union with God, but in such a fashion that our works are the fruit of this same union and bear the light and love of God.

> Our activity, therefore, springs always from a source within us, after the manner of Christ, who at all times worked with the Father in such a way that the Father dwelt in him and himself did the works. In this way, we will follow Jesus in the hidden and humble life of Nazareth, either praying to the Father in secret, or obediently labouring in his presence.[5]

Chapter 33[6] summarizes this doctrine:

> How, then, can we fulfill our role in the People of God of being living sacrifices acceptable to God, if we allow relaxation and immortification of life, distraction of mind and useless conversation, vain cares and trivial occupations, to separate us from the Son of God – from him who is life itself and the Supreme Sacrifice; or if a monk in cell is held captive by a miserable anxiety arising from love of self? In simplicity of heart, then, and in purity of mind let us strive with all our power to fix our thoughts and affections continually on God. Let each be forgetful of self and what lies behind, and press on towards the goal to win the prize which is God's call to the life above, in Christ Jesus.

These few citations represent only a small sample. You can find others for yourselves (look where it speaks of interrupted prayer, etc.). But for the moment they are enough to indicate the concern that our Statutes have for the interior work of the heart and the intimate and utterly hidden union with God which it enjoins.

1. Statutes 1. 6. 16.
2. Statutes 4. 33. 2.
3. Statutes 1. 5. 3.

4. At no. 5 (Statutes 1. 5. 4).
5. Statutes 1. 5. 7.
6. Statutes 4. 33. 3.

CONFERENCE III

'Behold, I stand at the door and knock;
if any one hears my voice and opens the door,
I will come in to him and eat with him,
and he with me.
He who has an ear, let him hear
what the Spirit says to the churches.'

Revelation 3:20, 22

God is so close to us, around us, in us. The wind that caresses
our face, the bird that sings, the mountain touching the
heavens, an exquisite flower among the rocks, the immense sky,
silence that trembles in its fullness, a smile, a look of love – all
speak of the creator, *infundens esse*, leaving everywhere the
marks of his passage. And ourselves: he is the source of our
being and is more intimate with us than we are with our own
souls. But he is not an impersonal force. He has a name.
His name is the Father, the Son, and the Holy Spirit. He is
communion in knowledge and love, the gift of his infinite self.
He seeks our response. He desires our love freely given, because
it is not love unless it is free.

'He who has my commandments and keeps them, he it is
who loves me; and he who loves me will be loved by my
Father, and I will love him and manifest myself to him.'
(John 14:21)

In the last conference we reflected on the importance of
sustaining the presence of God throughout the day, above all
by the repetition of ejaculatory prayers as a positive method to
assure watchfulness of the heart, the doorway of contemplation.
This is the common heritage of all monastic spirituality, but it

has been particularly developed by the Eastern tradition, above all in the hesychast tradition.

Hesychasm is a Greek word that conveys tranquillity, silence, stillness. In the monastic tradition it entails every aspect of the Christian hermit life from the physical flight from human society to the very mystical 'elimination of thoughts'* regarded as a surpassing means towards the goal of union with God, prayer without ceasing. As Cassian says: 'the totality of life, all the movements of the heart (*omnis voluntatio cordis*) become a single-hearted and uninterrupted prayer' (Conference X, 7). There is, therefore, an internal and an external *hesychia*, the first disposing us towards the second. The practice of solitude is essential to hesychasm, so that the two words hesychasm-solitude are almost interchangeable in monastic literature. In fact, hesychastic spirituality is the spirituality of the person whose unique preoccupation is union with God in love.

For us this spirituality is not an Oriental curiosity, perhaps of interest to scholars, but lacking practical importance. Certainly outside of monastic circles it has never had a large audience. This is understandable: the eremitic life in the West has only ever been of interest to a small minority. And the aspects of monastic spirituality regarding community and work found greater illumination in the West than in the East.

Nevertheless, if we look carefully, and if we pay attention to the transposition of terms arising from the differences in language, we find in the West the same great spiritual concerns, at least where the idea of the contemplative life remains alive.

As regards hesychasm,† the perfection of the human person resides in union with God by means of continual prayer. Pray always (Luke 18:1), in all seasons (Ephesians 6:18), without ceasing (1 Thessalonians 5:17); these recommendations are embedded in scripture and should be taken literally. We are not

---

* 'Solitude et Vie contemplative d'après l'hésychasme' by I. Hausherr, *Spiritualité Orientale* No. 3; and the other writings of this Father who is well versed in this subject.

† *Dict. de Spiritualité* ('Jesus' – 'Prière à Jésus') c. 1127ff., and 'Garde du Coeur', 'Hésychasme', 'Erémitique'.

always able to engage in specific acts of prayer without interruption because this is physically and psychologically impossible. This means that we must strive for an approximate state or a permanent disposition of heart, which, in a certain way, beyond the acts that flow more or less frequently from it, can be called by the name of prayer: the perpetual remembrance of God, the mysterious habit of the heart that is manifest as a form of virtual prayer and constant contemplation, the expression of a love that always tends towards the beloved without distraction even when it must attend to something else.

In the beginning, the way that leads to the continual prayer of contemplation is called *praxis*, the path of the commandments that effects patterns of behaviour, purifies the heart from its faults, and helps it acquire virtue. The regular observance of the monk is designed to do this; but also to eliminate thoughts (*logisma*), hurtful thoughts or simply irrelevant ones that immerse us in forgetfulness of spiritual things, that turn us away from the remembrance of God. The origin of these thoughts lies in the passions, our attachments and the working of the powers of darkness. This disregarding of thoughts is effected by guarding the heart, called, once again, vigilance, or *nepsis*, a state in which the soul is wide awake, balanced, present to itself and God; vigilant, and alert so as not to be taken by surprise by the wiles of the enemy. Guarding the heart assures the intelligent practice of discernment of spirits.

One of the better ways to combat thoughts and enter the perpetual remembrance of God is meditation in the ancient sense, that is, rumination (often on a text of scripture) that will help to root a spiritual idea of beneficial attitude in the soul.

One special form of repetitive meditation is the practice of short, frequent prayers. In this way Arsenius* said untiringly, 'God, lead me in the way to salvation.' Apollo repeated: 'I have sinned like a man; like a God, have mercy.' Others: 'Lord, Son of God, help me'; 'Son of God, have mercy on me.' Cassian tells us the secret formula handed down from some of the most

---

* The Fathers of the Desert (4–5th century). See, for example, *The Sayings of the Desert Fathers*, tr. B. Ward, Kalamazoo: Cistercian, 1975.

ancient Fathers of the desert, (Conference X, 10), 'O God, come to my assistance; O Lord, make haste to help me' (Psalm 70:1) – we still sing this verse at the beginning of all our offices.

It was St Augustine who first used the phrase 'ejaculatory prayers' to describe these formulas. In the East they speak of the prayer of the mantra, a prayer made from a single word or at least a single thought.

At the beginning of the fifth century, a privileged place began to be given to the invocation of the Lord Jesus and his name. For a long time the form of the prayer of Jesus was not fixed, but from the seventh or eighth century (the centuries of Hesychius of Sinai) the invocation began to take on a fixed form, or a number of forms that always centred on the name of Jesus (or, better, 'Jesus' by itself was the shortest form, and 'Lord Jesus Christ, Son of God, have mercy on me (or on us) a sinner' the most frequent form of the invocation). In addition, this invocation is co-ordinated in several ways with the breath: first in the sense that the remembrance of Jesus ought to be as constant as the movement of the breath. Later, we come to a technique that relates in a concrete way to breathing, that concentrates the invocation of the name of Jesus with the movement of the breath – but this, while a secondary development having real value, does not in itself touch the essence of the practice. We shall return to a very practical consideration of all of this, if you are interested.

For the moment we are able only to sketch the main threads of the Eastern tradition. I believe they are very consonant with our ideal in general, although they may need some adaptation to be useful for us. There is no difficulty in finding Carthusian authors who write and speak in the same terms.*

This seems to be confirmed by the names of the Fathers cited in the Statutes: Basil, Pachomius, Apophthegmata, Evagrius, Nilus, Cassian, Pseudo-Macarius, Benedict (who received the Eastern tradition above all through Cassian and Basil), John

---

* For example, Denys, *De profectu spiritus et custodia cordis*, Art. 4; Landsperge, *Enchiridion militiae christianae* vol. 4, ch. 16: see *Dic. Spir.* vol. 6, c. 111 and 112, 'Garde du Coeur'.

Climacus, Isaac of Nineveh, etc. Except for Basil, who reacted against the eremitic tendency in the Eastern tradition, all the others are, more or less, witnesses to the hesychastic tradition. Evidently there have been various currents running through this tradition, but we are considering only the major themes.

This all turns out as if, in seeking to amplify our own Statutes with those texts of the ancient monks that correspond to our way of life, we have inevitably rejoined the eremitic tradition of which we have been speaking, the Eastern primarily, but also the Western by derivation.

Let us recall that 'hesychia' is a tradition of quies, or peace, or contemplatio in Latin. We cannot be restrictive about these notions because in reality they signify different aspects of an integrated whole. Thus the word quies in the Statutes; the best translation in English minimizes the constant repetition of this word, which is a leitmotif of our Statutes (see the Fontes statutorum – 'Quies'), because the translator is constantly compelled to render it by different expressions as different aspects of quies come to the fore (repose, contemplative peace, tranquillity, contemplation, etc.). But it is also a good idea to translate hesychia each time with quies; the two terms describe the same reality with the same richness of reference.*

Here are some texts that illustrate the relationship between the ideal which the Statutes present, and the idea of the Eastern monks:[1] The cloistered monk

> who continues faithfully in his cell and lets himself be moulded by it, will gradually find that his whole life tends to become one continual prayer . . . In this way, having been cleansed in the night of patience, and having been consoled and sustained by assiduous meditation of the Scriptures, and having been led by the Holy Spirit into the depths of his own soul, he is now ready, not only to serve God, but even to cleave to him in love.

---

* See the study by Dom Jean Leclerc on the terminology of monastic spirituality of the Middle Ages. The different meanings of the word quies in our Statutes will be a source of intense study but that is outside our present concern.

A little further on it says that the fathers depend on the brothers 'to offer pure prayer to the Lord in the peace (the Latin is *quies*) and solitude of their cells.'[2] In other words, ours is the office of Mary who

> in stillness knows that he is God, purifies her spirit, prays in the depths of her soul, seeks to hear what God may speak within her; and thus, tastes and sees – in the slender measure possible, though but faintly in a dark mirror – how good the Lord is.[3]

Finally, there is a gloss on a quotation from Jeremiah that is one of the key texts for interpreting the contemplative ideal in monastic spirituality in the West: 'The solitary will sit and keep silence, for he will lift himself above himself,' expresses nearly all that is most desirable in our life: stillness (*quies, hesychia*) and solitude, silence and the burning desire for heavenly things.[4]

> The founding Fathers of our type of monastic life were followers of a star from the East, the example, namely, of those early Eastern monks who thronged to the deserts to lead lives of solitude (we can probably say '*hesychia*') and poverty of spirit . . . [5]

1. Statutes 1. 3. 2.
2. Statutes 1. 3. 5.
3. Statutes 1. 3. 9.
4. Statutes 0. 2. 6.
5. Statutes 1. 3. 1.

CONFERENCE IV

'Blessed are the pure in heart: they shall see God.'
Matthew 5:8

We have already spoken of purity of heart. It is worthwhile to try to determine the meaning of this expression a little more precisely, because there may be the risk that it is understood in too negative a sense: that it means on the one hand that one must love only God, or, on the other, that it might be understood in too restrictive a sense of chastity alone.

We all have our own ideas about purity: it is that which is without blemish, unalloyed, perfect. Perhaps in our imagination the word evokes the image of the innocent eyes of a child, the mysterious clarity of vision with which a young girl, guileless and serene, looks out on the world; a small flower that joyously displays its beauty one day; the sweetness of a bell sounding in the tranquil evening air.

These images help us to understand a little about purity of heart. But this purity is entirely interior; it is a quality that sounds the deepest places in us.

From time immemorial there have been those who have understood that the holiness of God requires a certain purity* on the part of those who wish to approach him. 'Be thou holy, because I the Lord your God am holy' (Leviticus 19:2). But when they were in thrall to fear they initially conceived of this purity in terms of external rites, taboos, prohibitions, such as were able to provoke the wrath of God. It needed much time and all the religious genius of the prophets before it was understood that this purity is interior, that it is purity of heart alone

---

* Note that the notions of purity and sanctity are very close.

that counts, and that this purity is contingent on love and not fear.

Christ leaves no room for ambiguity:

> And he said to them, 'Then are you also without understanding? Do you not see that whatever goes into a man from outside cannot defile him, since it enters, not his heart but his stomach, and so passes on? . . . What comes out of a man is what defiles a man. For from within, out of the heart of man, come evil thoughts, fornication, theft, murder, adultery, coveting, wickedness, deceit . . . All these evil things come from within, and they defile a man.' (Mark 7:18–23)

> 'The good man out of the good treasure of his heart produces good, and the evil man out of his evil treasure produces evil; for out of the abundance of the heart his mouth speaks.' (Luke 6:45)

> 'But I say to you that every one who looks at a woman lustfully has already committed adultery with her in his heart.' (Matthew 5:28)

The purity that Jesus demands is entirely unreasonable; it is a matter of the hidden heart that is known only to God that needs purification. What is outward only has value as a function of the intention, the heart, of love. What people think who are only able to judge what appears is not important.

We should avoid all that Jesus refers to when he reviles the Pharisees:

> 'Woe to you, scribes and Pharisees, for you cleanse the outside of the cup and of the plate, but inside they are full of extortion and rapacity. You blind Pharisee! First cleanse the inside of the cup and of the plate, that the outside also may be clean.' (Matthew 23:25–6)

It is the interior life, therefore, that we seek to purify, but it is not clear when we have reached the ground of purity. We must put ourselves in the school of God, where he pronounces

the beatitude of purity of heart in the Sermon on the Mount.
It must be placed in the context of the other beatitudes to
understand it properly, because the Beatitudes give shape
to everything, not in the sense of logical development, but as
variations on a unique theme, the same reality seen again and
again under its various aspects.

**'Blessed are the poor in heart, the kingdom of heaven is
theirs.'**

Matthew 5:3

The one whose heart is pure is also the one whose spirit is
poor. We already know that the heart signifies the very centre
of the person; the spirit of the first beatitude signifies the same
reality. The TOB* translates this beatitude, 'Blessed are the
poor of heart.' The New English Bible says, 'How blessed are
those who know their need of God.'

At the deepest level, to be pure of heart is the same as to be
poor of heart. The pauper possesses nothing; he can count on
God alone for everything. He accepts his poverty as a gift, a
reality that he experiences every day. We are essentially poor:
our bodies need to eat every day or almost every day; our bodily
existence is tied to a set of environmental conditions such that
the absence of one element causes them to suffer and die. We
receive our corporeal life as a marvellous grace in every
moment. Our existence is unimaginably contingent.

This contingency is in some way the image of our spiritual
destitution. Of ourselves, we can do nothing before God. We
can never give to God anything that we have not first received
at his hands. 'Apart from me you can do nothing' (John 15:5).
Nothing. Christ has said so categorically. We receive our life
from him as the vine-branch receives life from the vine. Separated from him, we are dead. We must graft this vital truth
deeply in ourselves. The virtue we practise sometimes is pure
grace, a gift of Christ, the life of his Spirit in us. 'What do you

---

* Texte intégral établi par les moines de Maredsous (Editions Brépols).

have that you did not receive? If then you received it, why do you boast as if it were not a gift?' (1 Corinthians 4:7). It is ridiculous to swell up with pride over a virtue or a gift. This is the reason that poverty is synonymous with humility; our humility is simply the truth of our poverty.

'For you say, I am rich, I have prospered, and I need nothing; not knowing that you are wretched, pitiable, poor, blind, and naked. Therefore I counsel you to buy from me gold refined by fire, that you may be rich, and white garments to clothe you and to keep the shame of your nakedness from being seen, and salve to anoint your eyes that you may see.' (Revelation 3:17–18)

'Blessed are the poor in heart' – Christ tells us – 'for theirs is the kingdom of heaven' (Matthew 5:3). The needy heart, its hands open to God. It does not put obstacles in the way. It presents the emptiness of its poverty before the infinite generosity of its Father. Its poverty makes it like God, because its capacity to receive is limitless. As the heart is always ready to receive more love and the spirit more light, God is not able to refuse it. Poverty is the door of blessedness, blessedness since Christ chose to become poor for us to transfigure poverty into divine abundance. 'For you know the grace of our Lord Jesus Christ, that though he was rich, yet for your sake he became poor, so that by his poverty you might become rich' (2 Corinthians 8:9).

We ought to be clear-eyed and loving in our acceptance of poverty. It is not that easy, however. It isn't easy to accept the inability of our soul to grasp God, the immense gap between our most exalted notions and the ineffable mystery of light. It isn't easy to relinquish all of our pretensions, all of our self-sufficiency, our sense of personal importance, our 'rights' before God. We are even prepared to go to enormous lengths to appear righteous before God, a righteousness that comes, just a little, from ourselves. One of the most difficult aspects of faith is to recognize that our own justification amounts only to rubbish, following the forceful statement of St Paul (Philippians

3:9) and that it is Christ who is our justification and our sancti-
fication – Christ alone.

> God chose what is foolish in the world to shame the wise,
> God chose what is weak in the world to shame the strong,
> God chose what is low and despised in the world, even
> things that are not, to bring to nothing things that are, so
> that no human being might boast in the presence of God. He
> is the source of your life in Christ Jesus, whom God made
> our wisdom, our righteousness and sanctification and
> redemption; therefore, as it is written, 'Let him who boasts,
> boast of the Lord.' (1 Corinthians 1:28–31)

If only we could understand this paradox: our poverty is our
wealth. You are familiar with that magnificent passage where
St Paul tells how, in spite of what had been revealed to him,
he was still tormented by a mysterious weakness:

> Three times I besought the Lord about this, that it should
> leave me; but he said to me, 'My grace is sufficient for you,
> for my power is made perfect in weakness.' I will all the
> more gladly boast of my weaknesses, that the power of
> Christ may rest upon me. For the sake of Christ, then, I
> am content with weaknesses, insults, hardships, per-
> secutions, and calamities; for when I am weak, then I am
> strong. (2 Corinthians 12:8–10)

Perhaps you begin to glimpse the sense in which poverty and
purity of heart are one and the same thing. Poverty, in its naked
reality, is only another aspect of the purity that wants nothing
but Love; that will allow nothing to get in its way, not even
itself, before the infinite outpouring of divine love. It wishes
only to be transparent to this love, a faultless glass through
which light pours undistorted and undimmed, without deflect-
ing the smallest ray by any imperfection.

Poverty, this poverty, is true blessedness. It is freedom from
that recurring anxiety of a perfectionistic personality that is
primarily concerned with its own affectation and never with
the grandeur of God; a freedom also from that fear that recog-
nizes clearly enough our misery before God, but is unable to

go beyond it with a faith that lays the foundations of our peace and hope beyond ourselves – not on the sand of our deserving, but on the rock of Christ. Because this blessed poverty is a poverty for love, the love of the one who loves and knows love in return. Who is poorer than the one who loves and who is richer? He receives everything completely gratuitously, he is utterly dependent on the Beloved who is his joy, he absolutely rejects his own resources. He knows himself to be nothing, but he has assurance that the gift he makes of this nothing gives happiness to the other. Our poverty makes God happy because it permits him to give us his love, and God wishes only to give himself.

Blessedness lies at the heart of this poverty of love because it is the pale reflection of the poverty of the divine persons at the heart of the blessed Trinity. Each person is fully himself through the gift of himself to the others. Their fullness is in their poverty; they are not diminished by their self-emptying.

'Blessed are those who hunger and thirst after righteousness, for they shall be filled.'

Matthew 5:6

The beggar who knows himself to be poor and accepts it is the same as the person who hungers and thirsts after righteousness (Matthew 5:6). He is a cry to the Lord: 'Create a clean heart, O God, within me' (Psalm 51:12) – a pure heart, upright, sincere, a heart of flesh that knows how to love. This heart can only come from him; God must create it in us; he creates it, that is to say, he makes it from nothing. He promises us a new heart.

'I will sprinkle clean water upon you, and you shall be clean from all your uncleannesses, and from your idols I will cleanse you. A new heart I will give you, and a new spirit I will put within you; and I will remove from your body the heart of stone and give you a heart of flesh. I will put my spirit within you, and make you follow my statutes and be

careful to observe my ordinances . . . You shall be my people
and I will be your God.' (Ezekiel 36:25–8)

When will we have a heart that loves joyously, simply, completely? When shall we become so united to God, so permeated
with his Spirit, by the Spirit of Love, that we become Spirit,
one heart with him, that we become, ourselves, Love? Love
that can come only from Love; to want a pure heart that loves
– this is to desire God, to thirst for the living God.

> As the deer longs
> for living water,
> so also my soul longs for you, my God.
> My soul thirsts for God,
> even for the living God:
> when shall I come to appear
> before the face of God?'
>
> (Psalm 42:1–2)

(The blessedness of pure hearts 'who see God' is the divine
response to this cry.)

> 'O God, you are my God; early will I seek you.
> My soul thirsts for you, my flesh also longs for you,
> in a barren and dry land where there is no water.'
>
> (Psalm 63:1)

(The realism of this physical desire is the corollary of the
realism of the blood and body of Christ given to us.)

This prayer of the poor, of the humble, resonates through all
the Bible, above all in the psalms. The power of the poor over
God is such that when it received its perfect expression in the
blessed Virgin, God responded with the gift that surpasses all
others, the gift of Christ in whom '. . . the whole fullness of
deity dwells bodily' (Colossians 2:9). The purity of Mary that
drew God to her is the purity of her humility and poverty, of
her thirst for God. Thus the joy of poverty burst forth:

'My soul exults in the Lord,
and my spirit rejoices in God my Saviour.
For he has looked tenderly on his humble* handmaiden . . .
he has exalted the humble and meek.
He has filled the hungry with good things . . .'

(Luke 1:46–8, 52–3)

Yes, 'all generations shall count me blessed' (Luke 1:48).
Once again, the beatitude of the poor.

The way is marked for us, the source of living water is given.
'Come to me,' says Jesus, 'all who labour and are heavy laden,
and I will give you rest . . . for I am gentle and humble in heart'
(Matthew 11:29). The source of living water – an interior
source, hidden and life-giving: 'If anyone thirst, let him come
to me and drink, and let the one who believes in me drink.' As
scripture tells us, 'Out of his heart shall flow rivers of living
water' (John 7:37–8).

This water of life is the Spirit: the Spirit of Christ that
transfigures us into the image of Christ (2 Corinthians 3:18),
the Spirit of adoption that makes us children of the Father
(Romans 8:15), the Spirit of liberty (2 Corinthians 3:17), the
Spirit of God that sanctifies us (Romans 15:16; 1 Corinthians
6:17), the Spirit of Truth that enlightens us (John 14:17); the
Spirit that dwells in us (1 Corinthians 6:19), that prays in us
(Romans 8:26), that marks us with its seal (Ephesians 4:30),
the Spirit that pours out love on us (Romans 8:26); the love of
humanity (1 John 3:24) and the love of God, in the intimacy
in which the Spirit ushers us (John 14:15–26).

The Spirit is given; we have received it, we have become
'soaked' in it (1 Corinthians 2:13), and yet we still have to
welcome it until it has permeated the utmost corner of our
heart. God respects our freedom and the integrity of human
nature. He allows us to grow slowly in his Spirit, according to
the degree of our receptivity. This is the ineffable drama of our

---

* The word that is translated by 'humble' (*tapeinōsis* is part of the vocabu-
lary of the *anawim* (the poor) and according to certain scholars is better
translated as 'poverty'.

life, a drama of love in which the lovers seek each other, often in darkness (see the Song of Songs).

God needs nothing of our wealth. But he does need our poverty, through which, alone, we may receive his gifts, his love, himself. God is not able to be himself, to be love, if he is not able to be self-outpouring into our hearts in the extravagant folly of his gratuitous love.

Treasure, therefore, your thirst for the living God.

One of the most beautiful definitions of a monk is that he is a man of desire. This restlessness does not allow him to be content with what is created; the thirst for the absolute, this hunger for love, is the wellspring, the impetus for his search for God. The day when he feels full to overflowing, he ceases to be a monk – and is living an illusion. God never surfeits us with the gift of himself but creates in us an ever larger capacity for love and, having done this, he replenishes us with a desire, a thirst, more ardent still. And it will always be this way with God for eternity without end, because God is without end. If we arrive at the end, it is not God.

CONFERENCE V

'Happy are those who weep: they shall be comforted.'

Matthew 5:5

Happy are those whom the pleasures and honours of the world
cannot satisfy. Happy are those who suffer the constraint of the
thirst for the God of love. They will be fulfilled. Happy are
those who weep, they will be comforted. They weep because
they do not possess that for which they were made. They lack
the one thing that could truly satisfy them; they yearn for the
One who carries, who is, this consolation in his own person.
'Come, Lord Jesus' (Revelation 22:20). Come quickly.

Tears* flow because of all that blocks the way to Christ in
our hearts, our sins above all, our petty selfishness and our
failure in generosity. Let us weep because the tears of repentence wash these stains from our hearts and make them ready
to receive the guest who will not delay. 'I stand at the door and
knock' (Revelation 3:20).

---

* To avoid misunderstanding let us distinguish between exterior tears and
those in the depths of the heart, the interior tears that they signify. It
is these interior tears, primarily, that we are considering when we speak
of 'tears'. In our culture, the physical expression of weeping is extremely
reserved. This attitude is appropriate for many situations that call for
control of our superficial emotions, yet questionable on just as many
occasions when it tends to choke our deepest feelings. In this matter
we have very different attitudes from those of the ancients. The cultural
ideas have changed more than the psychology. The ancients wept more
than we do. They did not care what people thought in the way that
inhibits us. They demanded that God give them the gift of unceasing
tears. Nearer to our time, St Ignatius of Loyola, who had tremendous
strength of character, shed torrents of tears in prayer. And his contemporary, Philip Neri, the 'joyous' saint par excellence, burst into tears
while celebrating Mass.

These are 'the tears of things' – this something . . . this fragrance, that sound, that leech from our old earth, soaked in
such pain and sorrow . . . which has seen such beauty and such
ugliness, such innocence and such vice, so much kindness and
so much malice. She cries her suffering as she waits for the
kingdom, and whoever hears and becomes conscious of these
roots knotting deep into the humus of the earth, who is sym-
pathetic to her deepest sighing, – in such a person the same
grave and silent tears will also arise, but these are tears borne
by the breath of hope that never dies that the Spirit of Christ
secretly sustains, and that occasionally burst into joy that is the
laughter of life.

There are tears of personal suffering, purely and simply, in
all their reality of bitterness and oppression. Actual suffering,
physical and psychological, can be ugly and disfiguring. Here
we touch the fundamental paradox of the gospel. These are the
people from whom we gladly turn our eyes, that we don't like
to think about very much. These are the people that appeal to
God's compassion; all these Lazaruses, with their stinking sores,
will be found in the kingdom of heaven when the final re-
ordering comes, the judgement of God and the reign of his just
mercy and eternal love. The last shall be first.

There are also tears that are not bitter. They are like the dew
of the morning, gentle, silent, springing from the depths of the
heart, we know not why. They do not have a name; they have
no cause. Sometimes these are tears of joy, a quiet joy, from
the depths, far deeper than our superficial feelings, tears born
from the silence of solitude when suddenly the life of stillness
takes on a luminous intensity – or rather, we become aware of
the intense reality of the life in which we are immersed. Why
weep? I do not know. Perhaps it is because of the utter gratu-
itousness of life, of being, which we experience in such
moments, like the occasions when we know what it is to be
loved, truly, deeply, for ourselves. Such a gift is so beautiful, so
grand! They are tears of gratitude, of wonder, of love. These
tears can be entirely interior, as they arise from the ground of
the hidden heart, or they may be exterior as well. It very much
depends on temperament and cultural conditioning.

We should not be ashamed of our tears, but we should avoid sentimentality and loss of control over superficial or unhealthy emotions, the releasing of tears of anger, of disappointment, injured pride, bruised feelings, of discouragement. There is a discernment of tears just as there is a discernment of spirits. There is a delicate equilibrium to be found. On one side, the solitary above all needs to be steadfast on the rock of faith, a steadfastness that extends to all of his feelings and emotions. On the other, he is like a little boat tossed about on every side by the changeable winds of his passions. He is lacking in stability and perseverance. At the same time, we risk self-seeking and becoming complacent even in our love of God.

To cite Père Lebreton:

> During the time of early fervour when God begins to draw the Christian to himself, he is intoxicated with this emerging love, and believes that the stronger his feelings the holier his response. This is a great illusion. St Teresa of Avila has warned us: 'We should shun these disturbances, and strive gently for self-restraint by calming the soul. This condition is like that of children crying so furiously that it seems they are about to be suffocated; their excessive feelings cease when they are given something to drink . . . Let this love be held within and not resemble the pot that heats up too fast and boils over because wood has been thrown indiscriminately on the fire.'*

These guidelines are very wise. To put them into practice is very difficult. Human beings addicted to their senses cannot afford the immense effort if they are not stimulated by the ardent flame of sentiment. This is the other side of the problem. To continue with Père Libermann:

> Man can only bring great tasks to fruition when his will is driven by passion . . . But it is impossible, in the wake of original sin, that the passions should be at the same time

---

* P. Lebreton, *Tu Solus Sanctus*, p. 75, quoting St Teresa, *Life*, ch. 29, 9 [translated by Kavanagh and Rodriguez, p. 192].

strong and completely submissive to reason. In conquering them reason extinguishes them. Only grace, and very great grace, can restore to man the integrity in which the passions may recover their right ordering, and their energy be entirely focused. (*Ecrits Spirituelles*, p. 550)

According to John of the Cross, it is this integration that is one of the goals of both active and passive purification which occur along the contemplative path. But just as for this uncompromising doctor, the practice of stripping and renunciation is not the only way-station before 'the senses are purified and the spirit is focused', that is to say, until we have recovered our lost innocence and perceive 'in every tangible thing, from the moment we notice it, the enchantment of a delectable presence and contemplation of God' (*Ascent*, Bk 1, Ch. 13). Thus, for the pure soul, everything, whether exalted or base, builds it up and purifies it more. But an unintegrated soul, because of its impurity, draws only evil from both. The hurtful propensity is already endemic within us; it is neither in presenting reality nor in our appreciation of it. Once purified, we recover the music of the Spirit and are able to become its instrument.

We should not quickly assume that this purification is complete; rather, from the beginning, it is helpful to understand that the goal is essentially positive. But the greatest purification comes through love and is given to us as the fruit of self-forgetfulness. If we are utterly transfixed by love, the heart's delight leaps towards the beloved without having to make an effort to avoid being attracted by other things, because everything is seen in the light of this love and everything reveals this love.

It is not necessary to condemn, or to numb the human heart. This heart has been redeemed by Christ, transfigured by his Spirit. It is the instrument on which Love plays the paschal hymn. Let us be human. A person whose heart is numb is not more human or Christian, but less so. Christ is not a plaster saint. He wept: over Lazarus, over Jerusalem, over the hardness of the human heart.

The ancient monastic tradition gives immense importance

to tears. 'Weep; there is no other way,' said Abba Poemen.
Compunction necessarily manifests itself in weeping, and compunction is one of the most fundamental attitudes for a monk.
It is an essential dimension of the monk's spirituality; a monk is
always someone who has a 'broken heart' (Psalm 109:16), who
possesses a conscience that is acutely aware of unworthiness,
of past and potential sin, of human weakness. This is the
secret of the monk's vigilance: sobriety and humility. And God
hears the prayers of the poor and humble.

Tears of repentence may be transcended by an expression of
the divine mercy, even though they spring from a certain awe.
But compunction does not fade. It remains, piercing the heart,
if it is the true compunction that arises from love: love that
weeps over its lost intimacy with God. To see God offended is
to see the divine image wounded in us; it suffers from the
unremitting discontent of a heart ever stretching towards the
ineffable.

The Church is not reluctant to put special prayers on our
lips to beg for the gift of tears. In our missal, we find the prayer,
Pro Petitione Lacrymarum:

> O almighty God, whose tender power brought, for your
> faithless people, living water from the rock; so draw from
> the hardness of our hearts such tears of compunction, that
> we may weep for our sins, and be made worthy to receive
> the abundance of your mercy.

According to the tradition, tears are the anointing of the
Spirit, a gift associated with the gifts of contemplation and
the gift of knowledge of the Holy Spirit. Moreover, in the
Eastern tradition, the monk who has never wept has never
conceived this knowledge. Gregory Nazianzen, John Climacus,
Gregory the Great, Cassian, the Sayings of the Desert – all
extol and explicate the gift of tears and specify the rules of
discernment required to distinguish good tears from bad.

There are tears that are always good: the tears of compassion
of one who knows that we share in the suffering and sin of each
person and all humanity, tears of love, tears of prayer: 'Lord
Jesus, Son of God, have mercy on us sinners.'

We know this powerful expression, marked by the Russian character, given solidarity by Dostoyevsky, through the mouth of Staretz Zossima in *The Brothers Karamazov*:

'Love one another, Fathers,' the elder taught (as far as Alyosha could remember afterwards). 'Love God's people. We are not holier than the laymen because we have come here and shut ourselves up within these walls, but, on the contrary, everyone who has come here has by the very fact of his coming here acknowledged that he is worse than all the worldly and than all men and all things on earth . . . And the longer the monk lives within the walls of his monastery, the more deeply must he be conscious of that for otherwise he would have had no reason for coming here at all. But when he realizes that he is not only worse than all the worldly, but that he's responsible to all men for all people and all things, for all human sins, universal and individual – only then will the aim of our seclusion be achieved. For you must know, beloved, that each one of us is beyond all question responsible for all men and all things on earth, not only because of the general transgressions of the world, but each one individually for all men and every single man on this earth. This realization is the crown of a monk's way of life, and, indeed, of every man on earth. For a monk is not a different kind of man, but merely such as all men on earth ought to be. It is only then that our hearts will be moved to a love that is infinite and universal and that knows no surfeit. It is then that each of you will have the power to gain the world by love and wash away the sins of the world by his tears . . . Each of you must keep constant watch over your heart and confess your sins to yourselves unceasingly. Be not afraid of your sins, even when you perceive them, provided there is penitence, but make no conditions with God. And I say to you especially – be not proud. Be not proud before the small, be not proud before the great. Hate not those who reject you, who defame you, who abuse you and slander you. Hate not atheists, the teachers of evil, materialists, even the most wicked of them, let alone the good ones, for there are many good ones among them, particularly in our own day. Remember them in your prayers thus: Save, O Lord, all who have no one to pray for them, and save those, too, who do not want to pray to thee. And add: it is not in my pride that I beseech thee, O Lord, for that, for I am myself viler than all men and all things.'*

This is the reason for solitude, silence and prayer: truly to restore the 'image of God' that is in us, to unite ourselves with all humanity in its most authentic truth – if only we love with a pure heart, then we conceive a consciousness of *this solidarity in which we are with all humanity in Christ*, the mysterious exchange of life that this entails, and our responsibility to effect it. Love is *essential*. The love of Christ in us bursts through the limitations of our individuality.

'Blessed are the meek: they shall inherit the earth.'
'Blessed are the merciful: mercy shall be theirs.'

Matthew 5:5, 7

We must never lapse into a notion of solitude, purity, and vigilance of heart that excludes compassion, in the sense of 'apathy', a Stoic insensitivity that passes for concern for human suffering. This is only the implacable egoism of a heart that shuts out everyone and everything. This is not the Spirit of Christ.

Those who say they love God and hate their brothers and sisters are liars; for those who do not love their brother or sister whom they have seen, cannot love God whom they have not seen. (1 John 4:20)

They *cannot*.

No one has ever seen God. If we love one another, God

* F. Dostoyevsky, *The Brothers Karamazov*, tr. D. Magarshack (London: Penguin, 1982), pp. 190–1. See also I. Haussherr, *Penthos*, tr. A. Hufstader OSB, Kalamazoo: Cistercian, 1982.

lives in us, and his love is perfected in us. By this we know that we abide in him and he in us, because he has given us his Spirit. (1 John 4:12)

The commandment we have from him is this: those who love God must love their brothers and sisters also. (1 John 4:21)

How could this poverty of heart that knows suffering, that thirsts for true love, how could it not become gentle and merciful towards its neighbour? It hears the Lord, who tells it:

'Should you not have had mercy on your fellow servant, as I had mercy on you?' (Matthew 18:33)

Be kind to one another, tender-hearted, forgiving one another as God in Christ has forgiven you. (Ephesians 4:32)

Without this compassion, our prayer is in vain.

'Whenever you stand praying, forgive, if you have anything against anyone; so that your Father in heaven may also forgive you your trespasses.' (Mark 11:25)

It is this sort of professional distortion that lies in wait for us, we, the monks who aspire to a very high ideal, who pass a lot of time contemplating this ideal in scripture and in spiritual books. Because of a very natural perversity, in the pejorative sense of the word, instead of recognizing how much we fail this ideal, we are struck by the imagined faults of our neighbours, and instead of forgiving, of humbling ourselves (because we are even more at fault), we judge and we condemn.

Before everything else, never judge anyone – anyone, inside or outside the monastery. It is you yourselves that you judge if you do this.

'Be merciful, just as your Father is merciful. Do not judge, and you will not be judged; do not condemn, and you will not be condemned. Forgive, and you will be forgiven; give, and it will be given to you. A good measure, pressed down, shaken together, running over, will be put into your lap.

For the measure you give will be the measure you get back.'
(Luke 6:36–8)

It is so simple!

We can find practical and affirmative application of this gospel stance in several places in our Statutes:

RECREATION

[At recreation,] Should a difference of opinion arise, let us know how to listen and to see the matter from the other's point of view so that in all things, the bond of mutual love will grow ever stronger.[1]

RESPECT FOR PERSONS

Since brotherly fellowship between men can never be perfect unless based on mutual esteem, it is certainly fitting in the highest degree that we, who live in the house of God, should bear witness to the love that comes from God by lovingly welcoming our brothers with whom we live, and by making a real effort to understand with heart and mind their characters and temperaments, however different from our own. For the source of hostilities, disagreements, and the like, often lies in contempt of others. Let us carefully avoid anything that could injure the blessing of peace; above all, we should not speak unkindly about one of our brothers.[2]

ADMONITIONS

'If your brother sins against you,' the Lord says, 'go and tell him his fault between you and him alone.' Now this requires very great humility and prudence, and if it does not proceed from that pure love, which seeks not its own good, it even does harm . . . . For the most part, it will be wiser to entrust our admonitions to the Prior, or to the Vicar, or to the Procurator.[3]

THE VISITATION

All can speak without constraint to the Visitors and put before them any matters, affecting either themselves or the community, that require a decision or advice. They may also make constructive suggestions for the common good. Before speaking of anyone else, we should recollect ourselves in prayer; for if we remain docile to the Holy Spirit we will be all the more certain of doing the truth in love. He who is truly at peace is suspicious of no one. It will often be better to keep silence rather than dwell on matters that are frivolous or cannot be proved, or on defects that are already being corrected.[4]

THE FATHER MASTER

While whole-heartedly zealous for the spiritual perfections of his charges, he must take care that he knows how to excuse defects in others.[5]

You can easily find other examples.

Blessed are the merciful: the person who holds the wretchedness of the other in the heart; the person who has compassion: that is to say, who suffers with the other. The silence of solitude is full of these waves of suffering and human misery. The prayer of the heart is most profound when we make it with sympathy, with receptivity, and when it is in tune with the faint murmur of humanity in its pain. Like Jesus on the cross: it is this compassion that gives birth to love that is willing to suffer and to heal through its wounds (Isaiah 53). Blessed are the merciful: for they will receive mercy. Not that they themselves will not have sinned, but their sins will be forgiven because they love much (Luke 7:47).

1. Statutes 3. 25. 13.
2. Statutes 4. 33. 4 and 5.
3. Statutes 4. 35. 5.
4. Statutes 4. 33. 7 and 8.
5. Statutes 1. 9. 1.

CONFERENCE VI

'Blessed are the pure in heart: they will see God.'
Matthew 5:8

All of what we have been discussing points to the beatitude of the pure in heart. Our purity of heart is always the Magdalene's purity. We are, all of us, sinners, and the word of God itself condemns us, if we deny it. 'If we say we have no sin we deceive ourselves, and the truth is not in us' (1 John 1:8). 'If we say we have not sinned, we make him [God] a liar, and his word is not in us' (1 John 1:10).

According to scripture, God declares that we are all sinners (cf. Romans 3:9–20). We all need to 'wash our robes in the blood of the lamb' (Revelation 7:14). It is the blood of Christ alone that can purify us (1 John 1:7, 9). It is by eating the Body of Christ that we are transformed into this pure flesh.

For me, the great joy of my priesthood, unworthy as I am, and – let's face it – impure as I am, is to be able nonetheless to offer to God the pure sacrifice of Christ: 'and from the many gifts you have given us we offer to you, God of glory and majesty, this holy and perfect sacrifice: the bread of life and the cup of eternal salvation' (Eucharistic prayer No. 1). The sin in us runs so deep that we cannot liberate ourselves except by dying on the cross of Christ for the sake of the new life of the resurrection.

> Therefore we have been buried with him (Christ) by baptism into death, so that, just as Christ was raised from the dead by the glory of the Father, so we too might walk in newness of life. (Romans 6:4).

I have been crucified with Christ; and it is no longer I who live, but it is Christ who lives in me. (Galatians 2:19–20)

It is by this means that this wondrous new life, announced by the prophets, is realized in us. It isn't so much that the law is changed; it is the heart itself that is changed. We receive a new heart, the heart of Christ by the gift of the Holy Spirit of Christ, the Spirit of Love. In him we turn with filial confidence to the Father crying, 'Abba!' in obedient love, and through him we love one another.

Something completely new is born: a new life is given us. The Christian's purity of heart is Christ's purity of heart. It is grace, freely given. It comes from afar. It is born from the wounded side of the crucified. It surpasses all our petty efforts, it surpasses even our desires because it is holy with the holiness of God and sets our human hearts on fire. It is an infusing fire that does not tolerate sin, limitations, unlove in us. It consumes, it burns, it purifies by the intensity of its light. 'Our God is a consuming fire' (Hebrews 12:29).

Of course there is Our Lady, whom God preserved free from sin in anticipation of the merits of his Son. This is only an apparent exception. Everyone needs to be redeemed and purified by Christ. Mary has a share in fallen humanity. She also needed to be purified, except that Christ's grace acted in a completely different way. She was preserved from every spot of sin, in light of her honour as the Mother of God.

Occasionally we find something analogous in certain people, who are called to a life of intimate union with God and who in a special way are preserved at least from grave sin, which is almost incredible, given the moral climate of our time. They bring God innocent hearts – innocent, because if it is only ignorance or fear, it is not a virtue. But these people are innocent because they know the beauty and value of human love and the created world. Theirs is the fruit of a clear-eyed and serious dedication to a higher love, even if it is not the absolute transparency of Mary Immaculate. But for all of that, it is a quality that is above all simple and joyous and evidences a purity of heart which is very lovely and engaging.

But even those who have received this grace must have no illusion that it is anything but grace, a free gift. Like everyone else, they have the potential for the worst excess, and in the final analysis, it is love alone that counts for anything. A sinner may be able to love more deeply than they do. The gospel affirms this again and again:

'A certain creditor had two debtors; one owed five hundred denarii, and the other fifty. When they could not pay, he cancelled the debts for both of them. Now which of them will love him more?' Simon answered, 'I suppose the one for whom he cancelled the greater debt.' And Jesus said to him, 'You have judged rightly.' Then turning toward the woman, he said to Simon, 'Do you see this woman?' [a woman of the town who was a sinner – v. 37 – who had bathed the feet of Christ with her tears and wiped them with her hair, who had covered his feet with kisses and anointed them with fragrant ointment] 'If I tell you that her sins, which were many, have been forgiven, it is because she has loved much, but the one who is forgiven little loves little.' (Luke 7:36–50 (in part))

Sin even figures in the divine plan of God's love; it is the *felix culpa*, the 'happy fault' that the liturgy celebrates and is the cause of Christ's inexhaustible grace that he has given us.

For if many died through one man's trespass, much more surely have the grace of God and the free gift in the grace of the one man, Jesus Christ, abounded for the many. (Romans 5:15)

We know that all things work together for good for those who love God. (Romans 8:28)

Everything, even sin, as St Augustine glosses this passage.

Just as there is a deepening humanity, a more loving heart, that the happy do not suspect, but that suffering alone can hollow out, so also there is a special quality, a particular intensity to surrendered and grateful love, that only forgiven sinners are able to know. The purity of a restored heart, the purity of heart of the Magdalene, has its own kind of riches. What it lacks in the exquisite clarity and spontaneous joy of the purity of innocence it has gained in humility, gentleness and humanity, because it better understands the frailty of the human heart and it does not demand its 'rights' before God – it doesn't have any and it knows this only too well. Christ loves to gather these people around him who are poor in virtue.

But practically speaking, there is hardly any purity that is entirely innocent, just as our first innocence is never entirely lost. Please understand me: I am not limiting myself to chastity alone. What is of interest here is purity of heart. Interior and exterior chastity, when it is both the grounding and the fruit of charity, is a wondrous song of love to God. As the Statutes say, 'it is a high gift of grace; it bestows an incomparable liberty of heart to find union with God in undivided love.[1] But when it is a mere refusal to love, when its sole preoccupation is maintaining an icy and implacable defence of its exterior virtue, it can be deeply wounding to this reality, without which it has no meaning, that is to say, love.

In order to avoid such an absurdity that can only result in an artificial isolation of chastity, I insist on the full and inclusive meaning of purity of heart that characterizes all of our personal activities. It is for this reason that I say that there is hardly any purity that is entirely blameless, because who among us has never sinned, has never failed in charity, has never failed in love in relationship with God and neighbour? And who knows if one such act of indifference, one such failure in compassion, one such act of injured pride, scornful contempt, impenetrable egoism, has not wounded love, wounded God, any more than the sins of the flesh of another?

When I say that innocence is never entirely lost, I want to try to explain an intuition of my own that is very difficult to put into words. In the first place, rarely is a human action so absorbing that undertaking it engages the entire person. Rarely is a person entirely absorbed in either sin or virtue. The truth of the self is always somewhat hidden until the moment of death. This is perhaps the most profound meaning of death in as much as it speaks the definitive word about our entire life.

(By the way, it is possible to say that one of the fruits of guarding the heart and of the monk's gradual growth into freedom is that one is able to be engaged more and more deeply in appropriate activity, and the capacity for such absorption expands more and more to encompass the whole person.)

But there is also a sense in which a person remains innocent even *in the midst* of sin. I know this is paradoxical, and without going any further than the Russians, above all, Dostoyevsky, who loves to extol the holy prostitute, it seems to me that this corresponds to a human reality. One could dismantle the paradox and distinguish between the sins of the flesh that arise from the undisciplined energy of the passions and that can leave a certain virginity intact, and the sins that are the fruit of a deep interior malice that is cold and that sullies the heart more completely. But the Russians, and perhaps the poet Rimbaud* also, want to go further, I believe, and they perceive a kind of innocence that is born precisely from the profound and utterly real experience of the misery of fallen humanity that opens it to the redeeming grace of Christ. For these people, the way to heaven passes through hell – at least in certain worst case scenarios. I don't know if they are right. In any case let us not flatter ourselves too easily that we have fully understood the mystery of the cross of Christ or of its power to give birth to new life where there is less than nothing.

We must never judge anyone; we must never lose hope, never; we must never compare purity with purity. We must never lay claim to the grace of Christ; we never assume it, proud and complacent in ourselves. In the end, all is grace, for the Virgin and for the Magdalene. And in practice, in each of us, we are both at once.

Purity of heart is purity of love. We are pure in the measure that we love. Love is always pure. Because God is love, love is purity itself. Everything that springs from love is good and holy. Everything that does not spring from love is not good. But even

---

* Cf. Olivier Clément, e.g., 'Purification by Atheism' in *Orthodoxy and the Death of God*, ed. A. M. Allchin, supplement to *Sobornost*, Vol. 1, 1971.

in this case, what we do seeks to take on the name of love; and to some extent there is always a certain love that motivates all of our actions. Except that this is love gone wrong, shackled, distorted; a love that disproves Love, because it doesn't want to accept the ordering of love by which each specific love finds its true place in relationship with substantial Love. Love originates all true love; cut off from Love, love is nothing but a body without a soul, an obliterated face, a non-love.

Purity of heart consists in loving conformable with Love, that is to say, conformable with God. Note well: it consists in *loving*. Too often purity of heart is spoken of as not loving this or that, as if it were some sort of barrier. (In addition, there is a danger of too great insistence on 'guarding the heart' of monks especially if it is wrongly understood.)

To be sure, we are very frail and we need to protect ourselves from our own weakness, cutting ourselves off from situations that might cause our downfall – temptations, etc. Purity of heart involves well-balanced vigilance and an appropriate self-distrust. These are indispensable, as we have already stressed. Nevertheless, the ideal ought to be affirmative. Our vocation is to love – not that we love less, but more. To love, firstly, God. That is clear because we use all our energy to focus our attention on him. But also on our neighbours, humanity, the entire universe, which we discover and love in the true reality of the depths of God.* And this love should radiate on the people we are given to meet and walk beside.[2]

> Now that you have purified your souls [= hearts] by your obedience to the truth so that you have genuine mutual love, love one another deeply from the heart. You have been born anew, not of perishable but of imperishable seed, through the living and enduring word of God. (1 Peter 1: 22–3)

Our love is the measure of our purity. It is better to be

---

* See the sayings of Staretz Silouan, e.g. in *The Monk of Mount Athos*, by Archimandrite Sophrony, tr. Rosemary Edmonds, London: Mowbrays, 1973.

stripped of all virtue than to fail in love. Love is the fire that consumes all the impurities from our inevitably imperfect deeds and leaves only the gold of charity. 'Charity covers a multitude of sins' (1 Peter 4:8). I was struck in the words that Cassian put on the lips of Abba Moses* regarding purity of heart, by seeing him give, as an example of the pure heart, Paul's magnificent hymn on love in 1 Corinthians 13:

> Love is patient; love is kind, love is not envious, boastful or arrogant or rude. It does not insist on its own way; it is not irritable or resentful ... It bears all things, believes all things, hopes all things, endures all things ...

Cassian says in effect: 'If you want a portrait of someone who has a pure heart, listen to this chapter.'

The hymn from Corinthians contemplates fraternal love, as does St John: 'Beloved, let us love one another, because love is from God; everyone who loves is born of God and knows God. Whoever does not love does not know God, for God is love' (1 John 4:7–8).

Sometimes we read in spiritual books that we must love God alone. This can be misunderstood. It cannot mean to say that we should not love our parents and neighbours and all humanity. This would go against the explicit commandments of God. It cannot mean to say that we shouldn't love the beauty of the many creatures God has created and of the whole universe, who bear the trace of the Divine Beauty who has created them.

It would seem that the true meaning of this expression is that we should love our neighbour and the universe in God, in the ordering of Love. And perhaps we contemplative monks especially can find in this saying an indication of the way that our love seeks primarily, but not exclusively, to touch our neighbour and the universe in the heart of God, where lies their true reality and their end.

And there is something else. God is not the object of our love alongside or on the same level as other things, things which

* Conference I, 20–21.

have been created. There is no competition between God and our neighbour. Love given to another does not diminish love given to God. To God in himself. To be sure, our energy for love has real limits. Our psychological capacity for concentration cannot encompass everything all at once. This is a common justification for withdrawing our attention from what is immediate, what is created, to focus it on God alone. And there is some truth to this. At certain times we need to focus our hearts as directly as possible on God. This is one necessity of love between persons, and this is one aspect of union with God characteristic of our solitary vocation.

But that is not to say that love and the attention we give to our neighbour distracts from the love given to God. God is the 'not other', according to Gregory of Nyssa. God is not there in front of me, distinct from me, beside my brother, distinct from him. He is not a subject limited to this or that, like me or my neighbour or anything that is created. God is Infinite, Being, substantial Existence, Love. God is in everything and everything is in God. I can only think of limited beings each of which circumscribes its own little space of being and is capable of being set in opposition to another. I cannot think of God. God is. That's everything, truly everything. God cannot be opposed to another. He is never beside himself.

And when I love my neighbour, in his living, limited reality, I love God, the Limitless, the Infinite. And, if my love is genuine, I love with the love of God. My love for my neighbour is the life of Love in me, its concrete realization. The essence of Love, the whole of God, is present in this love, and this love encompasses God. In loving this limited creature, precisely in the unique limitation of the personality, I love, I touch God. This fleeting, perishable act of my love mysteriously participates in the eternity of the divine love.

This is the essential meaning of Jesus' farewell discourse in St John's Gospel. The love that the Father gives Christ, he gives to us, and it is the principle of mutual love and unity among us (John 17), thanks to the Spirit of God in us (1 John 3:23–4).

Therefore let us seek to love more deeply, more sincerely,

without any thought of return for our selves, conforming to God, and for the glory of God. But for the love of Christ, by faithfulness to his blood shed for sinners and the redemption of the world, in order not to grieve the Spirit of Christ, who lives in us and who pours out his love in our hearts, let us love with all our heart, with all our strength, with all our mind. The rest is nothing. This is true purity of heart.

> In embracing a hidden life we do not abandon the great family of our fellow men . . . If therefore we are truly living in union with God, our minds and hearts, far from becoming shut in on themselves, open up to embrace the whole universe and the mystery of Christ that saves it. Apart from all, to all we are united.[3]

Let us understand the significance of our solidarity. It is marked with the cross. Suffering is found at the heart of love, and is its hidden face. The discipline of love may one day demand from us the sacrifice of what seems best in our hearts. Love has a paschal rhythm; this is its law. Birth only arises from death, and one only possesses what one has lost – really, uselessly and irrevocably lost – one only possesses it in faith, pure faith.

By way of an appendix, may I take the liberty of adding a page of Cassian on purity of heart, that recapitulates in a very biblical fashion what I have just set before you.

PURITY OF HEART

> Everything we do, our every objective, must be undertaken for the sake of this purity of heart. This is why we take on loneliness, fasting, vigils, work, nakedness. For this we must practise the reading of the Scripture, together with all the other virtuous activities, and we do so to hold our hearts free of the harm of every dangerous passion to keep it pure and in order to rise step by step to the high point of love.
>
> It may be that some good and necessary task prevents us

from achieving fully all that we set out to do. Let us not on this account give way to sadness or anger or indignation, since it was precisely to repel these, to destroy them in our hearts, that we would have done what in fact we were compelled to omit. What we gain from fasting does not compensate for what we lose through anger. Our profit from scriptural reading in no way equals the damage we cause ourselves by showing contempt for a brother. We must always relate our fasting, vigils, withdrawal, and the meditation of scripture and all these similar things, which are merely effects and consequences of our piety, to the principal end to which we must tend, that is, to this purity of heart which is nothing other than charity.

1. Statutes 1. 6. 15.
2. Statutes 4. 33. 4.
3. Statutes 4. 34. 1–2.

CONFERENCE VII

'Blessed are the pure in heart: they will see God.'

Matthew 5:8

Up until now, we have been speaking of an affective and moral purity. But in the Bible, the heart is also the source of our intellectual life.

What is purity of the intellect?

We speak of a pure intellectual, that is to say someone in whom the intellect predominates to the detriment of other human faculties. 'Pure' is taken in the sense of 'unalloyed'. In passing it should be said that the perfectly pure intellect does not exist. Look around a bit in this 'thinking machine' and you will find a heart and even, sometimes, an 'animal'. The Christian tradition and all religious traditions are in agreement that the gift of the vision of God is not promised to this chemically pure intellect.

No one can raise himself to God's level by the sheer force of intelligence. Intellectual strength is measured by the level of being, and humanity is infinitely lower than God. We can only have the knowledge of contingent, limited beings, who receive their existence from another. We laboriously decipher the little bit of truth incarnate in the beings that come our way – and we are not able to penetrate even their fragmentary truth to its ground. We succeed in raising ourselves a little higher and obliquely glimpse spiritual values – goodness, wisdom, beauty, etc. But this being who is Goodness, Wisdom, Beauty – *Ipsum esse subsistens* – in which all these perfections are one and the same – God, the source and ground of everything, who is eternally the source of his own being, is absolutely beyond the reach of our little light. As St Thomas said so succinctly, we are able to know that he is, we are not able to know who he is. To know that we know nothing is the greatest human wisdom, and it is to know God as unknowable.

The intellect alone cannot see God.

At the same time, we must not fall into agnosticism.* Thanks to the traces of the Creator that he has left of himself in his creation, we see if not the divine beauty, at least some reflections of it. Being, goodness, wisdom, beauty are found in God. We can see only a limited being, beauty only in part, and we do not know the form of this beauty in the purity of its fulfilment, infinite in God, where it becomes one with its being, wisdom and love. The law of analogy assures us that there is a resemblance between created beauty and uncreated beauty, but immediately adds that the dissimilarity is much greater.

This brings to mind the young Augustine and his passionate search for the divine face among created beings, who responded, 'No, we are not the God you seek.' (Sections 5–7 in the second book of the *Confessions* of St Augustine on the knowledge of God are among the most beautiful – happily, this passage is read at Matins on his feast.)

But God has come to engage humanity. God has intervened in history, has spoken through inspired people. But while revealing himself in human speech, God also remains hidden because no human language is able to convey the divine mystery. In the end, inspired words must bow to the law of analogy. They can only gesture towards the mystery of which they speak; they cannot fully disclose it.

Christ is the consummate revelation of God.

> Long ago God spoke to our ancestors in many and various ways by the prophets, but in these last days he has spoken to us by a Son, whom he appointed heir of all things, through whom he also created the worlds. He is the reflection of God's glory and the exact imprint of all things,

---

* Following St Bonaventure, 'faith professed in the darkness of contemplation, face-to-face with eternity, a luminous darkness that bears more light than obscurity'.

and he sustains all things by his powerful word. (Hebrews 1:1–3a)

'Whoever has seen me has seen the Father' (John 14:9). But wait! The eyes that see are not the eyes of human intellect but the eyes of faith. To contemplate the divine glory in the face of Christ (2 Corinthians 4:6) our eyes must receive an abundance of power, an ability to see in the dimension of what is seen. Just as our physical eyes cannot see an abstract truth, so the eyes of our human intelligence can see God only if they receive other light, a light that is participation in the divine light because no one can see God except God. No image, no intermediary can make him known. God must unite himself to our intellect, we must become God, in a certain sense, so that we may see with his eyes, and yet it is we who see, if we are to see God.

This is the blessedness promised to us, but it will be realized only in heaven. Here on earth, we walk in faith. We have already received the fundamental power to see, our participation in the divine nature (2 Peter 3:4). God dwells in us; we are united with him in the essence of our soul. Our acts of knowledge and love touch him as he is in himself, but as 'in a mirror, dimly' (1 Corinthians 13:12), concealed under the veil of faith as if under a cloud. Our knowledge must pass through intermediaries less exalted than the divine reality, that are able to reflect only a fraction of his splendour. These intermediaries are the concepts of the faith that are always subject to the immutable law of analogy, as we have said of unlikeness, which nonetheless is able to touch God in the dark. (St Augustine speaks of 'the hands of faith' that hold Something in the night.) The other intermediary is our love for God. The impulse of love which the Holy Spirit infuses into us is able to break the bonds of our concepts and immerse us directly in God. In the still depths of the divine abyss, which remains hidden from our eyes, there is a sublime experience of God that is beyond speech, and far beyond conceptual knowledge.

Faith is 'the conviction of things not seen' (Hebrews 11:1). It speaks to us of an order of reality that is unfamiliar and transcendent, when compared to the order accessible to our sense and our reason which is placed at an infinitely inferior level.

Because God is wholly Other. God's true reality is utterly unknowable to us, and this unknowability is specifically divinity. We must consent to dwell in utter darkness, to relinquish our habitual ways of knowing so that it becomes possible to touch another reality, a world of which we have, literally, not the least idea.

Is this, then, purity of intellect? To walk in pure faith, to set aside all our sure knowledge (because it cannot be other than a created thing), to surpass all imagination, all thought, to wait patiently in stillness and utter emptiness, sustained by nothing but the obscure light of faith and the power of love? Certain schools of mysticism say yes. For example, Evagrius and Denys the Areopagite teach this, and it is recapitulated by John of the Cross. It is the way of pure prayer of the East. But let us go softly! There is a lot of wreckage along this heady way that should arouse a certain prudence. 'Man is neither an angel nor a beast, and his misfortune is that when he wants to become an angel he becomes a beast' (B. Pascal). And as our Statutes assure us, 'The journey is long, and the way dry and barren, that must be travelled to attain the fount of water, the land of promise.'[1]

Let us aim as high as possible. It is our vocation. But let us be sure that our feet are firmly planted on the ground before we take flight.

Let us say this: purity of intellect can only be truth, that is to say, conformity of the understanding with reality. To engage divine reality, this purity is to be found in the perfection of faith, because faith alone can attain the supernatural world as it is. The pure mind is therefore the mind that sees and evaluates everything in the light of faith, and is led by it.

THE FAITH OF A HUMAN BEING

But it is the faith of a human being that is in question, faith lived as a human being, an incarnate mind, and thus frail. It is not faith lived by an angel. In the most intense moments of prayer that are more or less ecstatic, we can sometimes know what it is to pass beyond all mediation (or almost) to apprehend God directly. But these moments are brief: they are the lesser summits of a continual endeavour towards God. This effort must be rooted in the incarnate nature of the person and be sustained by activities appropriate to human dimensions. These intense moments of pure prayer are the fruit of a life entirely focused beyond itself, yet humbly acknowledging its real humanity, its true human condition.

The monastic life, with a healthy realism, takes people as they are and consolidates this human foundation with *lectio divina*, study, liturgy, community life, the struggle to be focused habitually in the presence of God. It is a whole life and a human life.

THE DEVELOPMENT OF FAITH

Faith does not achieve perfection all at once. A person receives being over time, growing slowly from infancy to full maturity. Purity of faith also is acquired through a gradual evolution. It cannot be rushed. Purity of intellect manifests itself differently at each stage of the spiritual life, and according to the way that the Spirit guides each person. It is a progressive purification that corresponds to the measure of faith. Let us see how this operates in general at an ordinary level.

THE FOUNDATION OF OUR NATURE

Grace works in nature. A mature intellect endowed with certain powers of perception and reasoning is the very raw material offered for the Spirit to work on. To know how to organize its thoughts, to learn habitually to transcend the level of the senses, at the level of intellectual understanding and spiritual values, to have become sensitized by some contact with human grandeur and with human thought in its most illustrious exponents in the past, is already a tremendous asset for a person and enables one to live at a higher level and facilitates access to the ineffable.

Let it be understood that by the word 'intellect' I mean not only reason, the power of reasoning which is precious, yet inadequate when dealing with higher values, but also intuition. Thanks to intuition, we have direct apprehension of realities, of being, of the first principles of truth, an appropriate sense of ourselves, a lively conscience, the heart of a person that opens to us in confidence and love, and aesthetic and spiritual values. The intuitive powers of the intellect are infinitely more delicate and go infinitely further than reason, which does not, after all, do more than order what the intuition learns so that it can be used. All good education should nurture these higher qualities, but above all the education of a contemplative, because it is precisely on these intuitive faculties and an awakened receptivity that the grace of contemplation most readily grafts itself, and infinitely develops them according to their own nature.

God knows very well how to bypass this intellectual formation with simple souls, but it seems that the work of grace is seriously hampered – at least in raising the level of life (setting aside the ground of the heart and the issue of personal merit) – if it does not at least find a clear and honest mind (even if 'backward'), in which grace can find a home. But all things being equal (and often this is precisely the question!) a certain culture of the mind almost always offers a richer earth in which grace may work. At least a certain minimum of culture. Beyond a certain point the beneficial effects decrease, especially if, through badly conceived education, one has been drawn away from the instinctive responses of the intellect and a certain freshness and simplicity of perception that is able to receive reality in its unvarnished truth (without interposition of sophisticated categories).

THE REALM OF FAITH

An exact understanding of the truths of the faith and of our moral obligations, a more profound understanding of the mystery of our religion, is able to integrate the gifts of our secular knowledge and extract meaning from listening both to the world's story and to our personal story, enables a deeper life of faith, more detached from error and superstition – in a word, greater freedom, because knowledge frees us from many fears and follies. Ignorance, at this level, is rarely holy, either in its origins (in so far as it depends on us), or in its consequences.

The Statutes are explicit on this point:

> First of all, lest we uselessly fritter away our religious life in cell, we should, at once with zeal and discretion, devote ourselves to studies fitting to us; and this, not from an itching desire for learning, nor from a wish to publish books, but because wisely ordered reading endows the mind with greater steadiness and provides a foundation for the contemplation of heavenly things. For they are mistaken, who think that they can easily attain to interior union with God, while having previously neglected the study of the Word of God, or later abandoned it altogether.*

---

* The negative side of this exhortation is found in the chapter on 'The Observance of Enclosure' (1.6.4 and 5): 'Great abnegation is required, especially of the natural curiosity that men feel about human affairs. We should not allow our minds to wander through the world in search of news and gossip; on the contrary, our part is to remain hidden in the shelter of the Lord's presence.' 'We should therefore avoid all secular books or periodicals that could disturb our interior silence' (. . . above all, politics!).

Even in regard to the problems of the world and the great intentions of the Church, the Statutes suggest a certain discernment, leaving each to follow personal grace. 'Let each one, therefore, listen to the Spirit within him, and determine what he can admit into his mind without harm to interior converse with God' (1.6.6). 'Our concern is to be seated at the feet of the Lord to listen to his word' (1.6.5). 'To listen to his word' is our study, our *lectio divina*. The aim of these cautions is to ensure the interior silence necessary for this listening.

Intent, then, on the rich substance of truth rather than the froth of words, let us scrutinize the divine mysteries with that desire to know which both springs from love and in turn inflames love.[2]

LOVE'S DESIRE

The last phrase touches on a theme that exceeds any question of utility. The thirst for understanding is born of love. When we love something, we are never weary of knowing it better. Gradually, as we more clearly perceive the face of infinite Goodness, our love becomes more intense and more authentic, and drives us on in our search for understanding ever more deeply. This impulse is without end, because the mystery of God is infinite. It will not cease even in heaven when we are face-to-face with God. We will move ever more deeply into the infinite abyss of his mystery for all eternity.

THE ECONOMY OF FAITH

The desire for knowledge is another consequence of the economy of faith. To be sure, the human mind, made for light, for knowledge, for understanding, in its very nature is driven to search and is always seeking this light and therefore, even without knowing it, seeking God. But this inclination is unimaginably strengthened in us by the life contained in the seed of grace lodged in our souls. 'In fulfilment of his own purpose he (the Father of Lights) gave us birth by the words of truth, so that we would become a kind of first fruits of his creatures' (James 1:18).

Faith, then, is a hidden participation in the knowledge that God has of himself. It is a light that makes it possible to see God in himself, and that already touches him directly, even under the veil of verbal formulae that our understanding can but feebly penetrate.

Thus, faith is necessarily desire, desire nourished by the indwelling presence of God in the soul. This desire dwells in each person whom God has freely called to himself by name. It tries all possible ways to find intimate union, union of heart first and foremost, but also union of mind with God who is Spirit, whose life is an exchange of knowledge and love, and this communion of life with him is, in the same way, also an exchange of knowledge and love.

Personal knowledge: not only of the facts 'to do with God', but knowledge born of the reciprocal gift of self in *love between persons*. To share in another's purposes is one aspect of this communion. And God has revealed himself and his thoughts to us in scripture and in each one of us by the grace of the living presence of his Spirit. All of our study should be ready and loving attentiveness to his Word in us and in the inspired words of scripture. The teaching of the Church and the development of theology are only the preservation, the transmission and mediation of that which God makes known to us about himself.

Christ has called us his friends precisely because he has revealed the mystery of the Father to us. He has spoken in human words. He addresses himself to our intelligence. But even his discourse contains a mystery that surpasses our ability to understand. Yet we have every reason to believe that he wishes us to share with him in the knowledge of the Father, to the fullest extent possible, and to this end, he has given us his Spirit (John 14).

But these words, these concepts, obscure more than they reveal. We remain far from our goal. We would like to go beyond this laborious travail fragmented into ideas. Novice contemplatives in particular would like instant elevation to mystical union with God, and in their unfocused enthusiasm, most fail to see the need to go by this route. Sooner or later the 'law of incarnation' will come into play, and the personality that is not harmoniously integrated with the mind but is unenlightened or repressed will assert itself with a force that risks shattering a fragile spiritual and psychological equilibrium. Just as it is rash to aspire to union with God without submitting to the purification of ascesis, so it is a rash wish to jettison the supportive framework of doctrine.*

The discipline of doctrine is the first step towards conforming our spirit to the Spirit of God. But there are traps on the way, and there is purification to undergo.

We know that the essence of faith is neither what can be stated nor even fragments of truth: it is a Person towards whom we are moving through all of this. But it can happen that the movement of the soul stops; spiritual impulse becomes mere technique. It becomes 'at ease' among the ideas in which it has enshrined its faith,† and in this state it risks forgetting the radical inadequacy of created things and their dreadful disproportion before the reality of God. It is great progress to have traversed the region of earthly means and to have become accustomed to heavenly ones. It is a very great danger to believe that now it is all nailed down, that faith is completely set out. Our ideas do not show us God, and the ideas of the faith do so less than all the others because they are directed towards the intimate mystery of God.

After a certain point, ideas become an obstacle. In their human form, static, rigid and corporeal, they are *our* ideas as much as and much more than God's. And again, apart from all their individual inadequacy, they are merely ideas and thus

---

* 'We are already foolish enough by nature without becoming so by grace.' 'I say that if these learned men do not practice prayer their learning is of little help to beginners. I do not mean that beginners shouldn't consult learned men, for I would rather a spirit without prayer than one that has not begun to walk in truth. Also, learning is a great thing because learned men teach and enlighten us who know little; and, when brought before the truths of sacred Scripture, we do what we ought. May God deliver us from foolish devotions' (St Teresa, *Life*, 13, 16, tr. Kavanaugh and Rodriguez, p. 94).

'A priest ought to be distinguished as much by his learning as by his life; because learning that is not lived makes a man arrogant, but life without learning makes him useless' (Synod of Aachen, cited by John XXIII, quoted in *Journal of a Soul*).

† We can learn something from the absolute refusal of certain Eastern religions that refuse to 'objectify' God in a concept, however pure and exalted.

a means of knowledge subject to absolute limits, which, accordingly, presents a barrier to the soul that God calls to go ever further. Subjective purification – of these 'imperfect ideas' – and objective purification – of human 'ideas' – this is work that must be done.

It is not a matter of wandering in a mental fog, nor the soporific vanity where 'one thinks nothing, wants nothing, and doesn't even wish to think of anything'. It is rather becoming truly one with God and truly engaging Someone. The most authentic sign of contemplation is precisely 'knowledge and loving attention' towards God. 'The soul delights in finding itself alone with God and in gazing on him with love, without any particular consideration.'* A sentence that conveys all the paradoxes of contemplation: no longer truths but Person, to an extent never before attained.

Little by little, obscurely, a 'universal' knowledge enters the soul. Universal, not because its notions and concepts are indeterminate, but because it is communion at a level that transcends the conceptual: it is knowledge and presence of God. It employs the purity of 'spiritual powers', that is to say, the powers of intuition and communion. Reason's house is empty, deprived of 'intelligible forms' before an 'object' more mysterious than ever. But the mind communes with God, a mind that is no longer anything but an intensely focused and receptive attentiveness. This communion simplifies and purifies the soul; it is the experience of Person. The spiritual impulse that it nourishes impels the person towards God, transcending the inadequacies of concepts that falter or partially falsify (they remain a hindrance, however, and exert a distorting bias).

For a time, conceptual thought undergirds and strengthens the impulse of the soul towards God. But the sad moment comes when the inadequacy of the representational aspect of faith is exposed in all of its deficiency, and little by little it falls by the wayside and is superceded, while the spiritual impulse is purified and strengthened by its obscure spiritual communion that at the same time bestows extraordinary intimacy. And it is

---

* John of the Cross, *Ascent of Mount Carmel*, Bk. 1, Ch. 13.

not some indeterminate divinity with which I am united but
the Persons of the Blessed Trinity, through Christ, in the Holy
Spirit, to the Father.

> 'Those who love me . . . my Father will love, and we will
> come to them and make our home with them.' (John 14:23)

> '[The Spirit] abides with you, and he will be in you.' (John
> 14:17)

Then we must ask, isn't the doctrinal dimension a provisional
state which we pass through more or less quickly? Does the
monk in his cell have no further need of this corporeal support?
The frequent citations in the Statutes caution us that we cannot
neglect study of God's word, without falling into error, *'nor
later abandon it'*. In the same way, the monastic tradition and
the reality which imposes itself on us all still leaves a place for
a more ordinary contact with God through the means of concept and signs in *lectio divina*, the liturgy, etc. There is certainly
a progressive simplification; there is less need of doctrine, quan-
titatively speaking, and its role is less informative than evocative,
although the beneficial effects of deepening understanding are
always possible and desirable.

Additionally, it is possible to distinguish (without separating!)
intense interior moments of prayer that go directly to the
Beloved, and life as a whole that is inevitably closer to the general human condition in many of its components. To enable
clear discernment and the priority of each thing, we need to
explore the tradition, which will be the next conference.

1. Statutes 1. 4. 1.
2. Statutes 1. 5. 2.

CONFERENCE VIII

'Blessed are the pure in heart, they will see God.'

Matthew 5:8

I don't want to present a history of prayer – elsewhere I have summarized the major themes, and I will give it to you soon. For the moment, let me offer a greatly simplified version.

Reading, meditation, prayer, contemplation are the principal movements of prayer. We find them in the Bible as they are so 'natural' to human beings who search for the will of God and enter his mystery.

The Fathers did nothing other than this, but they bring to their meditation all the intellectual wealth of philosophical and literary education without the slightest deviation from their passionate search for God and intimate communion with him. It is this essential unity that makes their work so valuable and gives them a very special savour.

The desert solitaries were generally simple people, frequently illiterate, but they cultivated unceasing reflection on holy scripture, above all on the gospels and the psalms, which they most often knew by heart. They strove, primarily, for prayer without ceasing, sustained by frequent, brief prayers, sometimes condensed into a simple formula. Their goal was purity of heart, which they identified with charity and pure prayer, the 'prayer beyond prayer'* that surpasses every sign and every word, that is total immersion in God, in the contemplation of the blessed Trinity. These timeless moments of pure prayer were usually brief. They were the most perfect fruits of their ascetic life, of their life of prayer – in a word, of charity.

This vision of things does in fact correspond with the view

---

* Cf. Isaac of Nineveh.

of most of the desert solitaries. But some of them, more learned and imbued with philosophical notions, especially Neoplatonism, sought this pure prayer even more directly for itself, so to speak, and they conceived it in terms of intellectual purity (that is to say, the elimination of all images and concepts to throw themselves into the divine unknowing), rather than in terms of moral and spiritual purity (which they thought of as occurring at a lower plane). Evagrius is of this school of thought, for example. According to Father Hausherr, even they never applied their own theory, but in practice followed the way of compunction, purity of heart and ejaculatory prayer. In the meantime, the aspiration that they had formulated had tremendous influence on the course of the mystical tradition of the Church.

We find the same aspiration and the same intellectual intransigence in the Rhineland mystics, John of the Cross, etc. The hesychast quest for interior silence is in the same tradition. The monastic tradition followed the practical path of the desert solitaries. The basic spiritual food was to be found in meditation on scripture, or *lectio divina*, and in the liturgy that very quickly acquired a consistent framework and provided biblical food in digested form, that is, texts chosen for the liturgical year and conforming to the usage by which the Church read scripture. There were certainly times of private prayer, but they were not legislated. The liturgy, an extended period devoted to *lectio divina*, and the freedom to go into the church for private prayer as inspired by the Spirit, was the typical formula for the monks of the Middle Ages (see St Benedict, for example). But what is more important to notice here is that their meditation, prayer and contemplation are not states that are more or less exclusive of one another and allotted to various categories of persons (beginners, proficients, 'the perfect'), but rather different interior moments during the same time of prayer. This harmonious unity is well described by Guigo II in the *Ladder of Monks*.

Reading is the careful study of sacred scripture. Meditation is the pondering of deeper truth hidden from reason.

Prayer is the focusing of the devout heart towards God, which banishes evil and makes way for the good. Contemplation is the exaltation of the soul, ravished by the taste of eternal joy.

Reading seeks the ineffable sweetness of a blessed life, meditation perceives it, prayer asks for it, contemplation enjoys it. This is what the word of the Lord tells us: 'Seek and you shall find, knock and it shall be opened to you.' Seek through reading, and you will perceive through meditation; knock by praying, and you will enter through contemplation. Reading carries food to the mouth, meditation chews it and digests it, prayer extracts its flavour, and contemplation is the sweetness itself that gladdens and refreshes. (Ch. 2 and 3)

Reading, meditation, prayer and contemplation are so inextricably linked together and support each other in such a way that the first two are pointless without the latter two and one rarely or never reaches the latter without the former. For what is the use of reading if having chewed and digested, we cannot extract all its sweetness? Or if we are not able to go beyond this to the ground of the heart? . . . In the same way, what is the use of seeing, by means of meditation, what we ought to do if we are not strengthened by prayer that enables the grace of God? . . . What is fruitful meditation? That which causes fervent prayer to flower, which is ordinarily the way to the sweetness of contemplation, which only rarely or miraculously comes to us without prayer. (Ch. 12–13)

There is something very healthy, very natural in this way of living, because the problem is this: it is a question of a life, a whole life, that takes people as they are and seeks to integrate all their faculties in such a way as to respect their natural physiological rhythm. The monastic situation makes considerable space for solid nourishment, for the deep rooting of faith in the intellect. But the intellect is not cut off from the heart, from the life of prayer. It continually yearns towards the One who has spoken to it through the Word whom it glimpses obscurely. It moves quite naturally into prayer and, God willing, into contemplation. Then it falls back again to an earthly plane and gently begins the process once more with reading, etc. And all of this takes place within one practice: *lectio divina.*

In the following centuries, in the high Middle Ages, the process changes. In the twelfth century a reflective spirit emerges that places a high value on philosophical and scientific reflection that wants to analyse and classify everything. This finally results in a split between a dry rationalist theology and a spirituality cut off from its intellectual origins that is impoverished in content and wisdom, increasingly concerned with pure affectivity and morality.

Later, an innovative concept of religious life appears with orders dedicated to an apostolic purpose (Jesuits, Dominicans, etc.). At the same time, there is a concern to teach prayer to the laity. In addition, the time given to prayer becomes relatively short during a day already overloaded with various activities. It became necessary to have a method of prayer that would focus the mind instantly and energize the will for the entire day. People became preoccupied with correcting their faults, acquiring virtue, and doing good works. This is 'practical prayer' as it came to be called in the sixteenth-century Society of Jesus, prayer conceived as a function of the active and not the contemplative life, which is specifically ordered to enable union with God.

Moreover, the distinction made between the different types of prayer and between ordinary and acquired prayer, and infused contemplation, tended to harden into frank separation. Instead of understanding meditation, prayer and contemplation as successive aspects of the same prayer, they were regarded as different types of prayer to be kept separate, and assigned to various categories of seekers (beginners, proficients and 'the perfect').

Traditional prayer survived under the name of affective prayer. But while discursive meditation is isolated and schematized, affective prayer is cut off from its intellectual sources and is increasingly simplified until in the seventeenth century it becomes the prayer of simplicity and simple regard, which remains today the prayer of so many souls.

Certain differences from monastic prayer become immediately evident. Modern prayer is a fixed space of time consecrated to personal communion with God. Intellectual endeavour, rumination over the truths of faith have little place. Instead, people seek interior silence and encouragement in their love of God by extended acts of peacefulness that will not disturb interior silence. Meditation on a subject often appears only as a means of relief in the case of aridity or heaviness. This is a positive development in what it affirms, and rejoins the hesychast tradition in what is valuable in it, particularly if one is thinking of the time consecrated to personal, intimate prayer – at least this is the common perspective of modern authors. But if one applies this approach to all of life without distinction – and in my judgement, this is to misunderstand at least the greatest of modern spiritual writers – it rests on an acutely impoverished foundation and does not integrate the whole human person with enough realism.

Intellectual work plays a large part in traditional prayer, but so does prayer and direct conversation with God. To pray is not only to think of God, but also to speak with God. And it follows that to encourage love, the mind too must be fed, and perhaps this aspect of prayer has been somewhat too much forgotten.

This is important for us whose essential vocation is intimacy with God. We need a sufficiently broad base to support the entire day, and not merely a half-hour or hour a day. To support a whole life and not merely a weekend retreat, or a month's, or even one or two years. And we need to be rooted, sinking foundations deeply enough through our own nature that we can survive the aridity of the desert, and that even in the rarified atmosphere of pure faith, our humanity may flower. In a word, if the essence of the spiritual life is a personal relationship of love with God, it is a relationship with a Person who is (apparently) absent and invisible, and we need constantly to look for the signs of his presence, principally in his Word, to give substance to the bonds that unite us to him.

One of the differences between the ancient point of view and the modern one is that the ancients applied themselves to the study of mystical contemplation, whereas moderns objectify different degrees of mystical prayer. Mystical contemplation is not, in itself, a special degree of prayer. It is a transaction, and a more or less enduring one at that, involving the gift of wisdom most especially, the sort of experience of God in love that unites us to him, but not necessarily linked to the form of prayer known as mental prayer. God is able to infuse it just as well in the context of other forms of prayer such as the divine office, or even during manual work.

Mystical prayer, on the other hand, is the highest degree of mental prayer in which the soul is more or less in the contemplation that is mystical exchange. The degrees of mystical prayer are more or less measured by the degree to which this mystical exchange is complete, but the descriptions of different ways of mystical prayer include psychological elements which are incidental to the nature of mystical exchange (delight, suffering, soul's journey, etc.) and it is chiefly these elements that hold the attention of modern authors, for example, Teresa and John of the Cross (sixteenth century), when they describe the characteristics of each degree of prayer.

This independently marks progress in the discernment of spiritual things. But these distinctions frequently run the risk of creating rigid stereotypes in the minds of disciples. And this is in fact what happens in subsequent centuries: little by little mystical contemplation in itself comes to be seen as a category of mental prayer in the same way as discursive meditation and affective prayer. And while these latter were considered as two degrees of 'ordinary prayer', mystical prayer qualified as 'extraordinary prayer' and, during the eighteenth and nineteenth centuries, became more or less suspect – at the very least, the person who deviated from discursive meditation or affective prayer was considered a visionary.

Practically speaking, the ancient and balanced ordering of meditation and prayer towards contemplation and union with God is appreciably diminished. Contemplation is no longer perceived as the heart of the spiritual life in its totality, the hidden dimension of all its activity, but, on the contrary, it is viewed as an extraordinary sphere, inaccessible to normal life. Those who aspired to it risked living too much like angels, lacking the stability of a humane equilibrium grounded in the ineffable over the long haul. And modern spiritual writing with its penchant for psychological description risks encouraging self-absorption; attention is altogether excessively fixed on the self. It brings to mind the saying of the Fathers: prayer is not perfect as long as there is conscious prayer.

It seems, thus, that while benefiting from everything in modern development that is real progress, it is in our best interest to remain faithful to the ancient tradition. The modern shift in orientation is linked to new forms of religious life, while monastic life, particularly Carthusian life, preserves the structure and goals of perennial contemplation.

Human beings do not change essentially, at least, monastic human beings don't. That is to say, humanity in its natural simplicity and truth before God. The solitary is necessarily this sort of person: solitude requires it. It is with some reservation that we Carthusians welcome this tendency towards psychological analysis that characterizes the modern mind, because it risks obscuring, a little, the limpid quality of our intimate relationship with God. But it is unrealistic to think that we can escape it entirely, and in the event it has some positive aspects, as we are able to see in the case of Teresa of Avila.

Mystical aspiration, the unswerving impetus that does not wish to stop at created things (as such) is not to be denied or suppressed. On the contrary, our solitary vocation makes no sense at all if it does not exist in a perspective that sees beyond what is created. For us, the word finds its perfection only in the paschal mystery of silence. Only, to facilitate the leap into the divine abyss of self-forgetfulness, the monk needs the confidence of feet planted firmly on the earth, knowing that all of his being participates harmoniously in the effort. We have already seen that to over-objectify, to over-materialize faith in concepts is fatal. The solitary avoids this shoal for a living sense of the transcendent, the ineffable mystery of God that

impregnates every action and sign with adoration, with Euchar-
ist, penetrating ever more deeply in the heart.

All of this environment, even the mundane nitty-gritty of life,
is lived in this way: the immense spaces of living solitude that
permeate everything, the monastery itself, the prayer of its very
stone, the soaring nave of the church and the audacity of the
bell that would pierce the heavens, silence full of shadows and
gentle light, the invisible presence of past generations, whose
prayer hallows every corner, the monks who pass and smile
without saying anything, the mountains standing like sentinels
around the dwelling which they seem to look on with a certain
amazement, while doing their utmost to provide it with a framework that is always lovely and ever-changing.

> 'You crown the year with your goodness,
> Your paths overflow with richness;
> in the wilderness pastures it flows,
> the hills gird themselves with joy,
> the meadows clothe themselves with flocks,
> the valleys cloak themselves with grain,
> they cry with joy, and sing.'
>
> (Psalm 65:11–13)

Please excuse this little digression! What I want to convey is
that we ensure the particular nature of our vocation by a profound sense of the mystery of God – this great, infinite something that is hidden beyond everything we can say – however
legitimately – about God. Adoration and love alone are the key
to the kingdom where alone those who know their need of
God, who are immersed in silence, can enter, those whose
hearts have been purified of every image, every form, and who
are motivated with a nameless desire for the One who is beyond
every name.

The divine mystery is personal. It is this that gives a special
character to the apophatic striving towards God. The life of
faith is a meeting with a Person – 'the hands that hold Someone
in the night'. Every encounter with a person is more a question
of intuition, of shared nature, of mutual discovery (except with

God: one must become God to know God), of love that goes beyond even our clearest perceptions. This engagement takes place on a non-discursive plane. It brings to mind St Teresa of Avila's aphorism on prayer: 'What is important is not to think much but to love much.'

Thus, it is intimate and personal prayer, this 'exchange of love where one meets one to one this God by whom one knows one is loved', that sustains living, personal contact with God.

But this feeling of being in the presence of a Person should permeate all intellectual endeavour. We should always be aware that through the concepts and words a Person is revealing himself, and leaving traces of presence. This is the theological principle of St Thomas.

> Now, whoever believes, assents to someone's words (someone who sees what we cannot); so that, in every form of belief, the person to whose words assent is given seems to hold the chief place and to be the end as it were; while the things one holds on that person's authority hold a secondary place.*

It is this personal end we must keep in mind when we study, when we read the Word of God, when we celebrate the liturgy, when we encounter our neighbours. 'When you have done this, you have done it to me' (Matthew 25).

This is the personal encounter that fills with presence the soul that is empty of concepts. Facing someone we love, by whom we know we are loved, the mystery of the personality does not trouble us. On the contrary, love discovers delight in it, because it has a presentiment of inexhaustible riches, and it rejoices even more in the measure that these riches surpass its powers of comprehension. 'Glory to God in the highest heavens.'

In one sense, the mystery is necessarily involved in personal love. The attraction of a woman is all the greater because she remains mysterious always, even in the gift of her whole self.

---

* *Summa Theologica* 2/2, XI, 1, c

There always remains a yet more intimate communion to desire.

In heaven, the mystery of God, precisely as mystery, will be our eternal blessedness. From the point of view of the intellect, too, this will be forever, the blessedness of poverty.

Here once more purity and poverty signify the same thing, because together they speak the language of love.

Purity of heart in its aspect of purity of the intellect is the striving of love towards the hidden Person behind the veil of words and signs. It is the desire for personal communion that always goes further to enter the purity of light without form in the solitude of a silence that surpasses all speech. It is poverty of spirit, pure receptivity before pure truth, that knows God is all in all, and that the two are one.

Deep calls to deep. (Psalm 42:7)

The Spirit and the Bride say, 'Come.'
Amen. Come, Lord Jesus! (Revelation 22:17 and 20)

CONFERENCE IX

'Blessed are the peacemakers: they shall be called the children of God.'

(Matthew 5:9)

This beatitude shows us another dimension of purity of heart because there is no purity of heart without peace. Purity is transparency, transparency is tranquillity, peace: like a tidepool in its clarity and stillness, that exposes for contemplation 'all the treasures that it contains, unblemished and dazzling, each in its setting: white pebbles, rose-pearl shells, seaweed and urchins with their intense colour'. Until a hand comes and troubles the water and everything is obscured, disturbed, confused.

PEACE

Rest, calm, tranquillity, the quiet bestowed by order (St Augustine). We all desire peace in the depths of our being. But often we ignore the nature of this good that we invoke with all our desires, and the paths we follow to obtain it. The false prophets of every age 'have misled my people, saying, "Peace," when there is no peace' (Ezekiel 13:10), that is, no true peace.

There is a false peace that is a lie, a more or less conscious self-delusion, a fixture of a closed and complacent ego, an escape. It is possible to enter religious life in order to flee life that is too hard for a poorly developed personality. This becomes the peace of the vanquished and is an illusion because in the cloister such a person will encounter the same struggles, the same challenges to maturity. We cannot escape our selves.

But there is an escape that is not a capitulation, but rather the consequence of a clear-eyed evaluation that makes an exact assessment of what the world can offer as compared with the sole Good, and that wants to be free of all that hinders its search for God. 'Therefore, my brother, flee all these concerns and miseries, and forsake the world's tempest for tranquil rest and safe harbour' (Letter of St Bruno to Raoul le Vord, No. 9). 'God gives to his athletes their longed-for reward for *the labour of combat*: peace unknown to the world and joy in the Holy Spirit' (No. 6). This escape is no more than the absolutely practical living out of the gospel invitation, 'So therefore, none of you can become my disciple if you do not give up all your possessions' (Luke 14:33) (No. 10).

This is not running away from struggle, but plunging into the heat of battle. 'Do not think that I have come to bring peace to the earth; I have not come to bring peace, but a sword. For I have come to set a man against his father, and a daughter against her mother, and a daughter-in-law against her mother-in-law; and one's foes will be members of one's own household' (Matthew 10:34–6).

It is not the facile peace of the world that Christ brings, but his peace. 'Peace I leave with you; my peace I give to you. I do not give to you as the world gives. Do not let your hearts be troubled, and do not let them be afraid' (John 14:27). Note well. It is when he is being given up to the cross that he gives us 'his peace'. Thus it is not an absence of suffering and struggle. It is something more profound. This is peace of heart: 'Let your heart no longer be troubled or fear.' This is the peace of a heart that lives in Christ. 'I have said this to you, so that in me you may have peace. In the world you face persecution. But take courage; I have conquered the world!'

According to St Paul's magnificent statement, 'Christ is our peace; in his flesh he has made both groups into one and has broken down the dividing wall, that is, the hostility between us . . . He has . . . created in himself one new humanity in place of the two, thus making peace . . . through the cross . . . So he came and proclaimed peace' – to all (Ephesians 2:14–17).

The Gospel of Christ is the 'gospel of peace' (Ephesians 6:15), 'the good news of the peace through Jesus Christ' (Acts

10:36). 'We have peace with God through our Lord Jesus
Christ' (Romans 5:1), 'for in him (Christ) all the fullness of
God was pleased to dwell, and through him God was pleased
to reconcile to himself all things, whether on earth or in heaven,
by making peace through the blood of his cross' (Colossians
1:19–20).

We ought to be aware of the deep significance of the peace
which the priest wishes on us in the name of Christ in the
celebration of the memorial of his passion, and that we give
one another. Upon the instrument of peace* is figured the
crucified, because it is the death of Christ that is the instrument
of our peace with God and among ourselves and in us. The
act of kissing this instrument and passing it to our neighbour
ought to be an act of faith in the efficacy of the mystery of
Christ, and an act of love. By embracing Christ we receive his
peace, and we communicate this peace to our neighbour. This
gesture is a prayer, one that is frequently found in the greetings
of the apostles: 'Grace to you and peace from God our Father
and the Lord Jesus Christ' (Romans 1:7). *Pax Domini sit semper
vobiscum*, my brothers. By saying these words before the altar
that bears the sacrifice of the body and blood of Christ, the
priest feels an immense torrent of peace passing through himself, flowing from its true source, the sacrifice of the cross, the
love of the Son. It is one of those moments in the life of a
priest when he is aware of his personal poverty and, at the same
time, of the infinite riches of the grace of Christ. If he were
utterly transparent, what efficacy the sacrament would have for
unity and peace!

– Lamb of God, who takes away the sins of the world, give
us peace – 'The blood of Christ, who through the eternal Spirit
offered himself without blemish to God' (Hebrews 9:14). This
is our peace and it is given to us by the Spirit. 'The fruit of
the Spirit is love, joy, peace, patience, kindness, generosity,
faithfulness, gentleness, and self-control' (Galatians 5:22). 'For

---

* In the Carthusian liturgy, a cross engraved on metal is kissed by the
priest at the altar during Mass, passed to the deacon, kissed and passed
on to the members of the community, in sign of Christ's peace.

those who live according to the flesh set their minds on the things of the flesh, but those who live according to the Spirit set their minds on the things of the Spirit. To set the mind on the flesh is death, but to set the mind on the Spirit is life and peace' (Romans 8:5–6), and (Romans 8:13–16): 'If you live according to the flesh you will die; but if by the Spirit you put to death the deeds of the body, you will live . . . it is that very Spirit bearing witness with our spirit that we are children of God.' 'For the kingdom of God is not food and drink but righteousness and peace and joy in the Holy Spirit' (Romans 14:17).

'For God is not a God of disorder but of peace' (1 Corinthians 14:33), and 'it is to peace that God has called you' (1 Corinthians 7:15). 'Agree with one another, live in peace; and the God of love and peace will be with you' (2 Corinthians 13:11), we are promised by the word of God. Let us therefore be the peacemakers of which the beatitude speaks.

> The meaning of the Greek word (*eirēnopoios*) that is translated 'peacemaker' or 'who does the work of peace' is difficult to determine because it is not found elsewhere in the Bible. Palestinian revisions render it, 'Those who establish peace' or 'those who pursue peace'. In the rabbinic sense, to pursue peace is to try to obtain it to incorporate it in oneself, so that its rule prevails around one. It does not, therefore, necessarily insist on the role of peacemaker, that is to say, someone burdened with reconciling enemies. (P. Buzy, commentary on St Matthew)

INTERIOR PEACE

Let us make peace, first of all in ourselves, because if we are not at peace in ourselves, we cannot give peace to others. 'Find peace, and thousands around you will find it also', St Seraphim of Sarov assures us. It is the same idea in spiritual parenting in the Eastern monastic tradition. The spiritual parent is a person who has peace in the heart, the peace of the Spirit of Christ, and who therefore is able to radiate this peace to others. But we can go further and say that this radiance is not limited to physical contact. We are a single body, we are so profoundly one in Christ that the peace in the heart of the solitary communicates itself mysteriously in an utterly hidden way to the whole Church, to all humanity.

It is notable that when St Paul speaks of this peace of heart he also speaks of the idea of the unity of the body of Christ and of love. Peace is the embrace of a pure love that does not have to be sought.

> As God's chosen ones, holy and beloved, clothe yourselves with compassion, kindness, humility, meekness and patience ... Above all clothe yourselves with love, which binds everything together in perfect harmony. And let the peace of Christ rule in your hearts, to which indeed you were called in one body. (Colossians 3:12–15)

You see, peace is born of love.

EVANGELICAL LIGHTHEARTEDNESS

We cannot be peaceful if we are restless, full of anxieties about sins, weaknesses, the future, friends, everything. By contrast, the gospel invites us to have a certain lightheartedness, a lightheartedness quite properly scandalous in the eyes of practical people, sufficient in themselves, accustomed to anticipating the future, planning for every eventuality.

> 'Do not disquiet yourself [note the word 'disquiet', the loss of *quies*, peace, *hesychia*], saying, "What will we eat?" or "What will we drink?" or "What will we wear?" ... your heavenly Father knows that you need all these things. But strive first for the kingdom of God and his righteousness, and all these things will be given to you as well. So do not worry about tomorrow, for tomorrow will bring worries of its own. Today's trouble is enough for today.' (Matthew 6:31–4)

Be like the birds and the flowers, which are entrusted to God's hand alone and by it are led to perfection.

St Paul echoes the Gospel:

> Rejoice in the Lord always; again I will say, Rejoice. Let your gentleness be known to everyone. The Lord is near. Do not worry about anything, but in everything by prayer and supplication with thanksgiving let your requests be made known to God. And the peace of God, which surpasses all understanding, will guard your hearts and your minds in Christ Jesus. (Philippians 4:4–7)

Do not lose any more of your time looking backwards: 'Jesus said to him, "No one who puts a hand to the plough and looks back is fit for the kingdom of God." '

We must forget the past and not disquiet ourselves over what may happen; we must live uniquely in each present moment, because the present alone has reality. We so easily risk losing the present reality for the sake of reminiscences of a past that no longer exists and in daydreams about ephemeral desires in a future that does not yet exist. To be in God, to live in God: this is being, living in reality, in the present moment because God there is neither past nor future but only an eternal present, full of being and joy.

Give us today our daily bread. May your kingdom come.

CONFERENCE X

'**Blessed are the peacemakers: they shall be called the children of God.**'

Matthew 5:9

The evangelical lightheartedness of which we spoke in the last conference is ultimately based on our faith in divine providence, which is all powerful and loving. Everything, good and bad, is in the hands of God, the all-powerful and merciful Father (2 Corinthians 1:3). He loves us, he cares for us.

'Are not two sparrows sold for a penny? Yet not one of them will fall to the ground apart from your Father. And even the hairs on your head are all counted. So do not be afraid; you are of more value than many sparrows.' (Matthew 10:29–31)

We must always see with the eyes of faith, that is to say, to see in everything the benevolent hands of the Father, which mould us into the image of the Son. Everything: our companions on the way, this frustrating circumstance, that gift, this weakness, that burdensome responsibility, this exquisite joy, the weather, the falling rain, this awkward request, that smile that warms me, etc. etc. We must only open our eyes.

The spiritual life is like a dance with a partner who has a fertile imagination and who leads. We must be alert, responsive to the slightest indication of his intention, supple, ready to adapt to the movements with which he woos us. Thus we are available, free from every preconception, wide open to the unexpected, unfettered from every tie, detached, ready to let go of everything without hesitation. We must not look for a way to halt this mobility and make it something fixed. We must never settle down into any place or with any thing. The monk is a pilgrim, an exile, a wanderer like Abraham. He travels light, without a lot of baggage, nothing but essentials.[1] He makes use of things – this is the human condition – but with freedom: he is not caught up in them, and he is not preoccupied with them. His Father knows his every need. In our day we have the habit of consulting specialists, qualified people. Well then, let us leave all of this to God. For our part, let us seek the kingdom. 'If the way to God is easy, it is because it is travelled not by loading ourselves with burdens, but by getting rid of them.'[2]

Getting rid of them: this is the secret of peace. Only the person who is poor in heart is able to enjoy interior peace, because this person alone is pure in heart. We must give everything, holding nothing back: time, preferences, personal attachments, mental preoccupation – and those of charity. It is even better if someone takes them from you; the gift is more pure. Do not refuse someone who imposes tedious work on you, who takes the book you are reading, who needs your affection, who imposes their will and whims on you, who abuses your good will, etc.

> 'And if anyone wants to sue you and take your coat, give your cloak as well; and if anyone forces you to go one mile, go also the second mile. Give to everyone who begs from you, and do not refuse anyone who wants to borrow from you.' (Matthew 5:40–42)

Because in all of this, we see the hands of the Father and, in our neighbour, the face of Christ (Matthew 25).

Here we come again to poverty of heart, which is the condition of our liberty, of our responsiveness to the slightest touch of the Father, that assures the conformity of our will with his, and in this way roots us in interior peace.

> Let us be constantly vigilant that there be nothing there (in our cells and our lives) that is superfluous or an affectation.[3]

The monk has elected to follow Christ in his poverty and by his poverty to be enriched. Depending on God and in no wise on things terrestrial he has treasure in heaven and it is there that his heart ever tends. [He recognizes] that he owns nothing.[4]

By his profession, a monk 'knows himself to be so much a stranger to the things of the world that he has no power over anything at all, not even over his own self, without the permission of his Prior',[5] in order that, 'set free from the world, [he may be] able to strive more directly towards perfect love'.[6]

Poverty aspires to liberty, which itself is in service to charity, which brings us into the peace of God.

Certain saints have a consciousness of being so completely between the hands of the Father that they are absolutely unable to preoccupy themselves with making provision for anything. They expect everything from God with a simplicity, a kind of *naïveté*, we might say, that is disconcerting, and this means that they neglect the most elementary human arrangements. I don't know if our faith is less than theirs. Perhaps it is the spirit of our times but we strive to do everything possible at the human level before asking God's help. A miracle belongs to the economy of the extraordinary and at its heart, from some points of view at the very least, it is a good thing. In the past, at least among average Christians, effective action on the human level to combat social and political injustice, etc., was all too frequently neglected. Victims of abuse were exhorted to see their condition as an expression of the will of God, and piously to accept it. What crimes haven't been perpetuated in the name of God! It's understandable why so many people have concluded that God is nothing but a tyrant. It's also understandable why the Church has lost almost all the working class.

God has given us intelligence and energy: let us use them to do what is in our power. For example, there was a young religious whose 'supernatural' spirit was held up as a model for us. This monk refused medication and surgical intervention to the point of death from appendicitis. He put his confidence in God alone. I wanted very much to concede the strength of his faith, but I was not at all edified. In my humble opinion, a profound faith in God, whose activity certainly is able to dispense with our co-operation when he wishes, and to play with the normal ordering of things, does not exclude our doing everything we are able to do as human beings. It is possible to say that faith in the incarnation of the Son of God requires us to include human gifts, because God visibly takes the order of creation terribly seriously. He subjects himself to its laws even unto death. The redemption of humanity was not effected by waving a magic wand but by the sweat and blood of a man. We are continually confronted by the respect of God for his creatures.

But more to the point, faith teaches us to live at a more profound level than human health and success alone. In the perspective of faith, what is good is that which pleases God and co-operates with eternal salvation, and what is bad is that which is not pleasing to God and imperils eternal salvation. This is a different criterion of discernment by which suffering and sickness may be seen as positive: 'Everything works to the good for those who love God' (Romans 8:28).

We must never lose peace. There is nothing that can come to us that is equal to that. If after doing everything possible the evil remains – there are many things, both within and outside ourselves, that we cannot change – why then add to the evil even more by losing our peace? And above all, for us contemplatives, we should lose an even more precious good, because interior peace is the indispensable condition for hearing the voice of God within. The delicate clarity and diaphanous light of intimacy can only be perceived in stillness, tranquillity, quietness. And these things that disturb us are insignificant in the light of the Eternal. They are transient.

Sometimes the wise of this world have successfully adopted an attitude of acceptance amounting to fatalism in regard to events and the laws that govern human life over which they have no control. This is one form of wisdom, but it leaves humanity at the mercy of an impersonal destiny and there is no room for free will.

The Christian submits to the will of a Person who rules and orders everything according to the plan of his love for humanity. Often the Christian, too, is unable to understand the meaning of incidents in the drama in which he is engaged. Sometimes he is shocked, wounded by what seems to be irreparable harm. He must have confidence in his Father, abandon himself to his will and believe in a redemptive outcome. 'Father, if you are willing, remove this cup from me; yet, not my will but yours be done' (Luke 22:42). There will be paschal moments: the whole point is to believe that this death in Christ gives life, eternal life without any darkness.

But in general, the Christian lives in a completely other world than that of the atheist carried along to a cruel and absurd end. Look on Christ: the peace that emanates from him and the source of his peace is the union of his will with the Father's. In everything he does during his entire public ministry it is his serenity that predominates, the serenity of the Son who walks attentive to the Father, who contemplates the work of his hands and does everything his Father commands. Nothing can disturb this source of living peace. For him, everything is love because everything comes from the Father.

Christ's chalice was bitter, his hour of triumph the hour of the cross. He knew it, he foresaw it, he accepted it for the love of the Father and humanity. He did not lose 'his peace'. Instead, it sprang from that suffering, consented to, redemptive; it flowed over us, he gave us 'his peace', his Spirit of loving obedience.

Do you wish to walk in life without succumbing to the dangers and weariness of the way, without falling victim to the frustrations and suffering that are inexorably a part of it? First and foremost, let us run with perseverance the race that is set before us, looking to Jesus the pioneer and perfecter of the faith, who for the sake of the joy that was set before him endured the cross, disregarding its shame, and has taken his seat at the right hand of the throne of God (Hebrews 12:1–2).

Our life is a paschal life: with the blood of the resurrection flowing in our veins, we run towards eternal joy, love has triumphed over death. For us, everything is hidden under a veil of faith. So then, our faith must be alive! Let us live like people who see the invisible, who are animated by the Spirit of God. Let us put our confidence in God to whom we have entrusted all of our being and all of our life and go forward towards the meeting with the unexpected that comes to us from God, from the hands of the Father. Let us allow ourselves to be carried by the joy of the risen and living Christ.

We must believe, we must accept the gift of life, to welcome life itself with the confidence and simplicity of a child. 'Let the little children come to me, and do not stop them; for it is to such as these that the kingdom of God belongs. Truly I tell you, whoever does not receive the kingdom of God as a little child will never enter it' (Luke 18:16–17). The child who with simplicity and wondering gratitude welcomes the gift of grace is the type of the poor of heart of the Beatitudes.

You remember that in the beatitude, the peacemakers are to be called the children of God. This is a beatitude that looks to the Father. And we are already his children in Christ. 'See what love the Father has given us, that we should be called children of God; and that is what we are' (1 John 3:1). From the depths of our being the Spirit cries, 'Abba, Father' (Romans 8:15). What trust we must have!

> 'Ask, and it will be given you . . . Is there anyone among you who, if your child asks for bread, will give a stone? Or if the child asks for a fish, will give a snake? If you then, who are evil, know how to give good gifts to your children, how much more will your Father in heaven give good things to those who ask him!' (Matthew 7:7–11)

We are invited to the feast of life. Let us enter without fear. Let us offer to the Lord the homage of our joy and confidence, the liturgy of our laughter. Life is a great adventure; the darkness of the future is the necessary space for the exercise of our liberty and our faith. We go to the Father, all together, children of God, brothers and sisters of Christ, heads high, with an unshakeable confidence and a joy that no one can take from us (John 16:22). In this light, all our little upsets and difficulties have small importance, they are beneath the dignity of a Christian.

Who will separate us from the love of Christ? Will hardship, or distress, or persecution, or famine, or nakedness, or peril, or sword? . . . No, in all these things we are more than conquerors through him who loved us. For I am assured that neither death nor life . . . nor the present nor things to come, nor powers, nor height, nor depth, nor anything else in all creation, will be able to separate us from the love of God in Christ Jesus our Lord. (Romans 8:35–9)

'O you of little faith!' 'If you knew the gift of God' (John 4:10).

To become truly aware of the miracle of the love of God and the grandeur of our inheritance in Christ silences all the murmurings of our conceit, our self-love, our ambitions, our fears, our dislikes, etc. Because it is the pull of our passions that undermines our peace, like strident, quarrelsome voices painfully shattering the stillness of the evening; what is prayer without interior silence? How can there be interior silence unless the voice of the passions is stilled? Without a holy indifference to our success in the world, to our reputation in the eyes of others, to our appearance, our health, our self love?

There is no peace without detachment. There is no detachment without effective renunciation.

There it is, the hard saying! Our passions carry us towards what is pleasing and delightful to us, towards what we love. Thus they cause us to avoid what is unpleasant and hurtful, the things we fear or hate. The way of resurrection is the way of death, a curtailment of life, a mortification of the senses, etc., etc. Today, as always, we don't want it. But listen to Christ: 'If any would follow me, let them deny themselves and take up their cross and follow me.' 'Naked, follow the naked Christ', said the primitive monks. There is no other way.

There are no shortcuts. But, we might say, I love life and everything that is beautiful and alive! So much the better, because it is a first step towards Love, it is a momentum which is to be properly directed and channelled, not to be stifled. 'Insensibility is the death of the soul and of intelligence, that precedes the death of the body' (St John Climacus). God is the

God of the living, not of the dead. Christians renounce all that is contrary to the will of God and his purpose for us. But this is the work of the living and not of the dying, that opens us to life, to the prodigality of life in the risen Christ, and the liveliness of the Spirit.

To be a people of prayer we must have something more. We must have interior peace, our eyes must continually be focused on a light that is wholly other, and closed to ordinary light. We must be detached in regard to everything that is not God or that is not transparent to God. We must have silence in order to listen for that which is beyond speech. We must enter into the fathomless depths of our being where the heart and the intellect are one at their root, where God touches us, where God is at work on the root of our being, giving us being, giving (by grace) to each the uniqueness of our own life, giving us himself.

For the moment I am above all interested in interior renunciation. Later, we will look at how the Statutes translate this into the concrete requirements of our life. But it is important at the outset to establish the approach and the goal that ought to govern our endeavours in order to avoid counterfeits. In the beginning, it's a question of seeing clearly. I will repeat myself a little because I want to look at the same problem under different aspects, which overlap to some extent. So much the better! In the end we will come to greater understanding. But that is for the next conference.*

---

* Note: in speaking of detachment I am afraid of giving too much importance to what is of little consequence. Certainly detachment from things is an essential element of the spiritual life. This does not mean that we are obligated to make a continual effort of the will to be detached. A continual preoccupation such as this is unhealthy and sometimes results in a negative attitude and bitterness that has little to do with Christian simplicity and joy. And, in the end, it puts too much emphasis on secondary matters. To be continually preoccupied with denying ourselves something is to feed the desire to possess and give it importance. The kingdom of God is not made of such things, 'not food and drink but righteousness and peace and joy in the Holy Spirit' (Romans 14:17). The true contemplative doesn't need to make a constant effort to

1. Statutes 3. 29. 5.
2. Statutes 4. 33. 7.
3. Statutes 3. 27. 5.
4. Statutes 3. 27. 1.
5. Statutes 1. 10. 12.
6. Statutes 1. 10. 1.

mortify the senses. Only love is necessary, the heart turned to God and the things of God; or rather, he realizes that things are leaving him and detaching themselves from him. He quickly forgets them, so fascinated is he with the discovery of the wondrous Mystery. Let us not be like the fearful people who, on the mountain, did not take their eyes from their feet for fear of stumbling and were thus unable to revel in the broad horizon and vast expanses. Let us be bold enough to be joyful. Christ, and the love of God, are worth this.

CONFERENCE XI

'Blessed are the peacemakers.'

Matthew 5:9

Interior peace requires detachment, a detachment that is expressed by silence and solitude, poverty and obedience, chastity and prayer. Everything in our life is geared towards opening wide the door of our hearts to the Lord, for us to sit quietly at his feet and hear his word, for us to be set free to live in intimate communion with him.

The difference between the emptiness of a yogi and that of a Christian is this: the one closes the heart to all passion and desire, thus seeking refuge from all suffering; the other turns all the power of the heart to the service of love, focusing the passions of the body and the soul, and directing their strength to the service of charity. The Christian never takes shelter from suffering, because the law of Christ is love: confronted with the misery of life and the suffering of others, love becomes compassion – and, inevitably, suffering. An *apatheia* that excludes compassion cannot be anything but the obduracy of pure egoism. The symbol of Christianity is not a sculpture of the Buddha, massive and immutable, but Love nailed to the wood of the Cross.

But let us look how this work of ordering the passions is done.

Our passions have a certain autonomy; they are oriented towards their own ends and they are activated when one of these ends appears to the senses or in the mind. At the same time, it is in our power to control them, to submit them to reason and the law of God. But this only can be done with tact, gradually, as one would tame a wild horse.

St Augustine has defined peace as tranquillity of order. When our reason and our will are surrendered to God, and our passions to our reason and will, the essential conditions of interior peace are established. Because of our sinful condition, this presupposes our ascesis (the will finds itself opposed by disordered passions in revolt, each seeking its own end without regard to the others); and also, to a certain extent, because of the human condition (the personality is constructed little by little, the higher powers assuming control over the lesser ones as the human person gradually develops). Social and moral human maturation is about establishing order. A religious rule is a powerful tool, with its regularity, its wisely chosen practices, and the support, the example and companionship of others. Grace works unceasingly through these means, because God is a God of order and of peace.

The goal is not the destruction of the passions but their rehabilitation according to a true priority of values. Grace builds on nature. To the extent that the goal remains unfulfilled, we must cultivate attentiveness, vigilance – the *nepsis* of which we have spoken, that watches at the door of the heart in order to turn away hurtful desires before they can even enter into the heart. 'Apatheia, impassibility, does not consist in not experiencing passions, but in not welcoming them' (*Philokalia*, 'Centuries of Kallistos and Ignatius').*

But this is accomplished over a long period. It is more efficacious to exorcise the problem by nurturing what is good. We must focus the energy of the passions and direct them towards the good, towards God. Modern psychologists tell us that we must sublimate the power of the passions, transforming them from lower, more sensual desires, to higher, nobler, more spiritual ones. The ancients knew this very well. 'The perfect soul', says St Maximus (*On Charity*, III, 93),† 1500 years ago, 'is the one in whom the very power of the passions is turned towards God.' There it is: peace, *hesychia*.

---

* See *Writings from the Philokalia on Prayer of the Heart*, tr. E. Kadloubovsky and G. E. H. Palmer (London, 1977), pp. 164 ff.

† See *Maximus Confessor: Selected Writings*, tr. G. C. Berthold, Mahwah: Paulist, 1985.

Every religion and every human being who has sought to live their life in all its fullness has discovered the need for a certain separation from the world outside in order to enter within the heart. This is evidently necessary to keep the attention from being distracted by other things while it focuses on the sole object that it wishes to examine more closely. All study requires this, and all prayer presupposes it to a certain degree.

But what interests us is something else entirely. It is a matter of the search for God, for the Absolute. Mystical experience is found in all major religions; they are unanimous in saying that such experience requires detachment in regard to every created thing (as such) and the going beyond every representation. God is Wholly Other.

It is this that is the final purpose of our solitude; it is therefore worth the effort to understand a little more exactly, because there are counterfeits of solitude-peace that are not available to Christians.

For example, yoga is a spiritual path of detachment that goes extremely far. It aspires to detachment from the senses, imagination, discursive reason, passion, egoism. To a certain degree it generates mastery over physiological and psychological functions, and integration of the personality. It is a wisdom tradition because it raises a person beyond the pull of desires and contingency, and this is its solution to the problem of suffering. One has only to look at the huge, peaceful immobility of the Buddha sculpture. It signifies the quiescence of all its powers; its perfection can be compared to dreamless sleep.

But in his depths, the yogi ends in defeat, because his blissfulness is locked in himself. His efforts succeed only in isolating his own essential being in order to have a direct intuitive experience of it. His goal is en-statis (as opposed to ex-statis) of soul that contemplates itself in its own essence at a level that lies deeper than the physical or psychological.

This is already a lot for one human being, a return to an infantile state of innocence, entry into the limbo of unbaptized children. The cords of desire and therefore of sin are cut, but there is no love (because love, too, is a passion to be overcome) and therefore no positive virtue. The disciplines of yoga are

able to obtain one of the highest forms of purely natural blessedness, but it is far from the vision of God. It creates a void in
the soul, and encloses the soul in itself, which creates a hostile
climate for mystical gifts (see the implacable rejection of 'distinct apprehensions' in the mysticism of St John of the Cross).
But even if it is logical within itself and conforms to the philosophical principles to which it subscribes, it excludes the experience of God, because either it treats the soul as a single monad,
an absolutely independent little world, outside of which nothing
exists, or else the soul is the Absolute (Brahman), God, and its
task is to free itself not only from its attachments to anything
else whatever (which is nothing but illusion – Maya), but even
from its own unique personality in order to be reabsorbed in
its source. It is not a question of union in love, because in the
end there is only the Self.

But equally it is possible for the void to create an open door
for all sorts of incursions from the unconscious and the
demonic (Matthew 12:43–5) – you remember the gospel par-
able of the spirits' return to the soul that is 'empty, swept, and
put in order. Then it goes and brings along seven other spirits
more evil than itself, and they enter and live there; and the last
state of that person is worse than the first.'

Everything depends on the motivation behind the ascesis that
creates the void. If one seeks a human peace, the enjoyment of
oneself in solitude and isolation, one may indeed find this peace
but one cannot go beyond it, or else one leaves the way open
to the destructive powers of the personality. There are very few
people who know how to maintain their psychological equilibrium in solitude.

The discernment of spirits is not always easy, because it is
possible to seek an egotistical peace that can easily be conveyed
in religious terminology. When we say that we are searching for
God, are we sure we know which God we seek?

This is of practical importance for us. One can be in the cell,
in solitude, quite content, but in reality far from God. How
can we avoid this?

The will and spirit, the heart of the monk, must be firmly
focused on God himself, the absolute Being who is Goodness

and Truth, on whom everything depends. The ascetical effort to create an emptiness, a listening ear, a heart that is attentive must be simply a response to the divine activity; it must be God who begins to silence the heart by infusing a hidden taste for an immediate presence, and gives it a glimpse of obscure light quite different from that brought by concepts and words, and enables it to divine the presence of a Person, who beholds, who communicates.

Sometimes certain beginners, having read a number of spiritual books and absorbed philosophical teaching on God's transcendence of all discursive knowledge, quickly come to the simplistic conclusion that we can know nothing of God and that we ought to remain before him with a mind that is devoid of images and ideas. They are then able deliberately to impose on themselves a complete vacuum that resembles certain aspects of mystical emptiness but is not the same. It is only an *absence*, a silence effected by the will in consequence of reason (and therefore by reason), and it does not admit the subtle intuition of the intellect, informed by faith, nor the impetus of authentic love that transcends all mediation to touch the beloved Person, that ensures the quality of *presence* essential to true 'emptiness'.

This is one of those situations where conceptual knowledge of the spiritual life far exceeds the person's development of the spiritual life itself, and the genuine abilities of faith and above all, love. We must have the humility to follow the activity of the Spirit and not wish to look for shortcuts.

This false emptiness is bitter and its fruits are impatience with oneself (and with God!), self-centredness, a critical spirit, and judgement of others. Thus the energy is brutally repressed without being assimilated, and looks for an outlet for its aggressive self-affirmation in outbursts of anger, excessive activity, miscellaneous compensations, etc. This is not the only cause of the impression of repressed and frustrated energy given by certain religious; it is only one application of the principle of repression, the refusal to incorporate the full human reality in the spiritual ascent. There are others.

All the great teachers agree: one must not depart from

meditation, the ordinary way, for as long as it is fruitful and helps us to focus on God, to know him and love him. It is only when the soul finds it impossible to profit from these means that it leaves them. The fundamental principle is always to follow grace to let the Spirit lead us, instead of wishing to impose our own way of seeing, which is fatally deficient and selfish. Many saints have never left a more or less discursive way, but that has not lessened their sanctity in the slightest.

For all, outside of prayer-time, a discursive element in the sense of *lectio divina* is always part of the spiritual life.

Each person has a name known only to God, each has this way to follow. For any particular person (and only particular persons exist) there is no higher or lower way. There is only the way traced by God for this particular person, and personal perfection consists in following this way with the greatest fidelity and docility possible.

The spiritual life and the life of prayer always grow into greater simplicity, and it is important that each person should consciously encourage this tendency by seeking simplicity and purity in life as in prayer. It is always appropriate to yield to moments of silence in prayer, to be silent in order to let God speak if he will. But when God acts more directly on the soul and ushers it into another form of knowledge and an experience whose nature is more passive (which is only the secret activity of 'ordinary' grace become conscious to a certain extent), that depends only on God and his plans for the particular person. Let each hear the voice of the Spirit within.

In this matter too we must be poor, we must be humble and trusting. Most of us are not strong enough for God to inundate us with manifest grace. We would become proud and claim it as our own; we would grasp the gifts instead of yielding to the Giver; we would lose the invaluable means of pure faith.

And who knows? The light of grace is so translucent and delicate that its presence in all its purity remains hidden, often unperceived. It is only when it passes through our sensibility that it becomes visible. The mystics consider ecstasy as a weakness of the body that is not yet completely in harmony with the Spirit. There are those in whose life everything is 'ordinary', simple, humble. But they radiate a certain peace, a certain joy. In such a person we can perceive a soul whose heart is so given to God that this condition is their deepest reality, but so 'natural' that it is not possible to pin it down in discrete acts. It is scarcely conscious of itself.

Is this the way that the monk 'becomes prayer'? Is this 'prayer without knowing that one is praying'? 'Pure prayer' that is therefore more a question of being than of 'prayer'? Is it a question of pure white light rather than a kaleidoscope of brilliant colours perceived through the prism of experience more sensible than grace? In its essence, what is prayer?

From these considerations let us remember that we must never judge or compare, or, above all, despise others, or believe ourselves superior, because we have received some gift of grace. The surest path through the wilderness of faith is that which is humble, hidden, stripped. Blessed are the poor of heart.

> 'For my thoughts are not your thoughts,
> nor are your ways my ways.
> This is the word of the Lord.
> But as the heavens are high above the earth,
> so are my ways high above your ways
> and my thoughts above your thoughts.'
>
> (Isaiah 55:8–9)

But let us come back to the path to the light. When a mysterious attraction makes it impossible for the soul any longer to be nourished by ordinary means of meditation, it must be quiet, attentive, listening for what the voice of God says directly to the heart. It is the moment of being an emptiness for God, an attentive silence of love. This is the good emptiness, hollowed out by God, created by Love.

It is perfectly normal that someone who lives continually in the presence of God, who does his will, who loves and knows he is loved by him, has an intimate and simple relationship with him. Such a person doesn't need lengthy pondering to turn towards God, nor many words to express faith and love. He will speak to the Lord with utter simplicity about his concerns, his wounds, his desires, etc. He will remain quietly in his presence, occasionally in the silence of a simple gaze of love and trust.

If God wishes, he can deepen his communication with the soul, inviting it to enter deeper in its heart, bypassing his ordinary way of operating for a yet more hidden way, more intuitive, more silent. Such a person is not afraid in spite of an initial impression of impoverishment and exile. Because it is precisely an exile, entry into a new sphere of existence. I have insisted sufficiently on the personal character of communication with God so that I can permit myself to use impersonal images as well. As with every notion that we apply to God, we use that of person in an analogical sense. God is person, but not in the sense of a human person, which is the only sort we can know directly. This is not to say that he is less of a person than we are; on the contrary, he is infinitely more. God alone is truly person. The human person is but a pale reflection, an inclination towards true personality, rather than a person in the full sense of the word.

Therefore, in order to convey other aspects of God-Person, it is sometimes necessary to have recourse to images in our experiences that are, or seem to be, impersonal. It is in this sense that I offer the idea of exile, the entry into another sphere of existence, to convey a more intimate approach to God.

We are familiar with a three-dimensional world: length, breadth, height. Suppose there is a being that is only aware of two dimensions, length and width. The world of this being is entirely conceived in terms of length and width, and it hasn't the least idea of the height of the realities that are right before its eyes. Suppose a superior being that has the capability of seeing and knowing in three dimensions of beings reveals to the lesser being the existence of the height of things – but speaking in the only language comprehensible to this being, that is to say, a language based on his experience of two dimensions only, and so trying to give some idea of the height of things by way of analogies with the length and breadth of things, and so very imperfectly. The astonishment of this being will be very great, and he will have the impression of an extremely painful exile. He will be constrained to believe blindly what the superior being tells him, because his faculties of knowing are incapable of directly perceiving the third dimension. He would be obliged to renounce his certainties, based on the evidence of his experience, in order to enter a superior world but as a stranger, utterly lost, exiled.

But let us suppose that the superior being has the power to give him new faculties of knowing, able in themselves to grasp the height of things. And that these faculties are able to be given him in embryonic state, their development being realized by progressive exercise.

This is the situation for the theological virtues of faith, of charity and hope that are infused in us by sanctifying grace. It is the same with the gifts of the Holy Spirit which ensure that these virtues operate in a divine manner closer to that of God.

In the beginning, the new vision of faith, so different from that of our bodily eyes and our intellect, seems to us to be but a shadow. We see nothing. It is only by exercising our faith, in judging and living according to this vision, that we become adjusted to its mysterious light and that we develop our new eyes. Natural light is so much more accessible that we must first close our eyes to its glare in order to perceive another light that is delicate and utterly other. When the eyes of faith are stronger and refined by the gifts of the Spirit, we are then able to look at the 'natural' world, but with a transfigured gaze that perceives a new dimension in it, its real identity, that sees the glory of God resplendent in the face of Christ and in the face of the entire cosmos, assumed in him and for him.

Let us not be afraid of the dark! It is the glare of the light that blinds us!

CONFERENCE XII

This entry into the deeper dimensions of reality is on a continuum with the ingress of natural intuition.

Incidentally, what is real? This flat earth, the utilitarian perception of things and of life, confined to subjective self-consciousness which alone exists in the positivist minds of so many modern people, is this world real? Or is this a deceitful mutilation of reality as, for example, the poet says, 'True life has gone missing. We are not in the world' (Rimbaud). 'I have a horror of reality. To tell the truth, I see nothing that is real, it is only a phantasm' (Nietzsche).

The world that we call 'objective' is only a convenience, a convention, an impoverished convention, the least real of all our fabrications. Nature is something else and we are part of it. We don't see it from the outside like spectators. A profound kinship unites nature and our soul. We bear the blame for the historic disaster that has given the advantage to the progress of individualism and the disjunction of the universal exchange of the empathy that exists in unity. We live further and further from the richness of the earth, the blighted life of a plant half cut from its stem. However, we retain an obscure memory of a lost unity; a presentiment, a face, the discovery of a flower allows us to glimpse it; it mingles with our enveloping unconscious, with its blessings and its terrors, it appears in our dreams under indistinct forms and masks.

But we have lost the key to this integrated life with the All. The seer, poet or mystic is its mage. Such people open for us from time to time the mysterious door beyond which lies the world in its deep reality and each being in its union with the Unity of All.

The interior gaze does not isolate us from the world. 'Every descent into the self, all interior contemplation is at the same time an ascension – assumption – to gaze at the true external reality' (Novalis). An innocent gaze beyond consciousness and sense brings us closer to the whole of reality by richer and surer paths than a closed perception and isolated concept. Interior and exterior dissolve into one. This gaze fills our hearts with everything that is, it reunites us to the vast universe, and we are able to speak of a vision, a whisper, a touch that brings from interior to exterior, a simple rootedness in the earth, in reality, truth, by virtue of contemplation itself. 'Close your eyes and you will see.'

The consciousness that is only turned outward is sightless and deficient. While momentarily turning inward, away from the first level of information provided by senses and intellect,* the 'I' is detached from neither the physical world nor its own carnality – quite the opposite: it collects itself in order to try to know at the same time as to be and to act with the whole of itself. To give attention to another I must begin with a time of interior silence, of reflection in the dark.

Attentiveness is not tenseness or strained effort but presence and relaxation, quietness and receptivity, presence with, love. Attentiveness can be learned. We can become sensitized to attentiveness. Everything that we have just said suggests that there is something to be seen. But how should we go about it? Is it self-evident that we know how to look, how to be so attentive that we discover the true face of things and persons?

Let us look at the process of attentiveness. It normally implies stillness of the body and a withdrawal, a curtailment of the mind that relinquishes other objects in order to focus on a single one. Focus and stillness. Attentiveness is the natural prayer of the mind that seeks truth. It is waiting, pure receptivity. It unconditionally welcomes the truth, whatever it may be. It does not interpose preconceptions, concerns or fears. The ineluctable conditions for attentiveness are an awakened mind that watches for the light, a thirst for truth, integrity and a brave heart, silence and solitude.

No single object seems real to us unless we give it a certain amount of concentration. Paradoxically, it is this attention that

---

* The concept of preconceptual experience sheds some light on this.

comes first, before the object. Which is to point to the great importance of cultivating the faculty of attentiveness. This attentiveness is linked to consent; it is always docile and completely acquiescent. We are forcefully drawn to choose that on which we project our attention, whether good or bad (1 John 3:2; Matthew 6:21) This is a law of our minds and underlines how important it is to focus on what will nourish the mind and not harm it.

Some obstacles in us to this attention are daydreaming (attention aspires to truth, and therefore reality; it is the mortal enemy of daydreaming, which is nothing but the projection and illusory satisfaction of our desires), sloth, egoism that sees itself reflected everywhere, the fear of truth and its consequences. We know how the monastic tradition insists on the necessity of a mind that is wide awake, sober, vigilant, pure. The contemplative ought eminently to be a person of reality, and if attentiveness stops at abstractions and daydreams, it does not come back to earth to disclose the depths of reality and the daily round, it fails to reach its goal. The kingdom of God is among us, here and now.

Age quod agis. Do that which you are doing. Attentiveness ought not to be confined to certain privileged moments, the time of prayer, for example. It ought to be operative in every moment. We must not drift through life as dreamers. On the contrary, we must apply ourselves, as far as possible, with the whole of our selves to what we are doing, at each moment. This is the secret of a fulfilled life, intense, rich, because each thing, each happening, each person offers us a wondrous richness if we will only pay attention. There is nothing insignificant, nothing banal; it is we who trivialize everything, merely skimming the surface with the tips of our fingers. We must practise doing everything with attentiveness, diligence and care. Even more, to the eye of faith, everything that is done for the love of God, in him, is important. We must be conscious that each person we encounter carries within a marvellous interior world, and attentiveness in love can be a way of entry and communion. And, to the eye of faith, my sister, my brother, is Christ. Isn't it worth paying attention? 'But, Lord, when did we see you?' (Matthew 25).

When you walk, walk. When you pray, pray. When you look, look. When you eat, eat.

The secret of life is quite simply to live it. The present moment holds inexhaustible richness. Attentiveness is the key to living profoundly. This depth is not confined to an esoteric sphere, but is at the heart of the daily round – precisely in its ordinariness.

There are several kinds of attentiveness depending on whether the attention is directed towards things, towards interior ideas and images, towards others, towards itself, towards God.

Looking at things: a house, a roof, a tree, a flower, the sky. Which is their real face? The one seen by the vacant passive eye, like a camera's lens? Or the face textured by the mystery of forms, by the dance of light and shadow, by the silence of a secret life, that artists evoke on their canvases? Isn't it the function of art to awaken us to the truth of things? And this vision is a communion. It reaches its perfection when interior sensibility is plunged in the same source from which all these beings come, when exterior sensibility resonates in harmony with the being that lives in them, to the point that it feels at one with them, with the flower, with the tree, with the sky – brother tree, sister flower! We have all had these privileged moments of intuition, of communion: the glory of the beauty of a tree set on fire by the rays of the setting sun, or the impudent smile of a little blue flower among the rocks and the snow, opens our eyes to see more or less profoundly. The aesthetic perception of beauty, and therefore of the reality of things, and the communion that it affords, are already great, and it is a good thing to open our eyes and educate our sensi-tivity. But there is a deeper gaze that comes from an even deeper attentiveness and communion. Passing over the particularity of each being, this gaze touches it in its very being, and finds itself one with it. It becomes all eye, all gaze, to such an extent that the subject is immersed in its seeing.

This may not be entirely clear but we have already encountered this grey area in the distinction between subject and object that is always found in higher forms of consciousness.

Zen Buddhism aspires to see the reality of a being from within this being. To see a flower truly demands that we become the flower, because, say the Zen monks, we are not something else. This represents an effort to pass through the screens of our feelings and the concepts that stand between us and reality. It is a focused gaze so innocent and direct that it isn't conscious of being the gaze of a person (who would take possession of it), but pure seeing, which becomes, if we dare risk the phrase, 'self-awareness' of the flower. Isn't this the ambition of the poet, to become the voice of nature, *its* interior voice? And perhaps this has a certain family resemblance with pure prayer.

Therefore, let us not disdain even the most ordinary fragment of being. Let us rather lend it our sensitivity and our voice to praise its creator. Is it partly because of this that we are on this earth? We are therefore responsible for the music of this flower.

We live in a world that is so rich, if only we knew how to look at it.

'I see his blood on the rose.'

Attentiveness to images and ideas. They are only the voices of reality in us, and therefore they cannot be separated from things. Sometimes in order to see greater depths of reality, we must abstract from direct engagement with reality and contemplate our semiotic systems. This is good, indispensable in fact, but it only takes us one step; the gaze has to take the results of this interior meditation on reality back to reality in order to illuminate it, and to be guided by it. If, on the contrary, the intellect is so fascinated with its own cleverness, if busy reason weaves more and more elaborate patterns, and thus becomes more and more removed from the sources of reality, it is unlikely that it has gained much in terms of apprehending the truth.

And we must not forget that reason, precious as it is, is not the only faculty of truth that we possess. Concrete experience, direct intuition, connaturality, love, are also ways that perhaps give higher access to truth, and are not to be neglected, above all when it is a question of the most mysterious realms of being (of persons, the truth of God, etc.).

The best environment for this sort of attentiveness is stillness, silence, a personal effort to understand that is not satisfied by second-hand reports and inadequately understood words, a humility which accepts the limits of its own powers of comprehension, and a sense of the mystery of reality.

Within the context of communion, attention to ideas is the most impoverished means of all, yet we must not forget that ideas, to the extent that they are true, conform our spirit to the Divine Truth and are a communion with God's Thought, and therefore with his Word. Christ is always hidden behind our clumsiest constructions, and the purity of his Spirit sometimes breathes through our stammering. Truth is prayer.

Meanwhile, we should distinguish between learning and knowledge.* Learning assumes an acquisition directed to concepts presented as a science that can remain external, and therefore does not lead to any change in the person. Knowing requires union of the knower with what is known, which is progressive and entails adaptation of the spirit and transformation. In the end it encompasses and transcends every conceptual category, even when it employs concepts, by a direct perception of Truth, Beauty, Being in themselves, and not objectivized.

Attentiveness to others. All attentiveness presupposes receptivity, presupposes faith, but the attentiveness that we bear towards others takes the most human form: a smile, our attitude that says that we accept the person before us as a potential friend and not as a potential enemy. It isn't a question of *naïveté* based on ignorance, of which life can soon disabuse us. It is a clear-eyed, steady regard of a person. It is not unaware of limitations and imperfections, but it penetrates beyond all that to the depth of the heart that is in each person, to the possibilities of goodness and grandeur that wait only for the inspiration

* The French is 'savoir et connaissance'. [Tr. note]

of trust and love to be realized. It is our failure to love that inhibits relationships.

Isn't this a fact of experience? When we come to know people a little more deeply, we discover unimaginable treasures and, frequently, we have the impression that the hidden fault is not the other's but ours.

Let us welcome each person as Christ, because in all truth it is Christ whom we welcome. 'You did this to me' (Matthew 25). Let us look for the beloved face of Christ in each person, for each is his true face.

APPENDIX TO CONFERENCE XII

WHAT IS REALITY?*

'What is REAL?' asked the Rabbit one day . . . 'Does it mean having things that buzz inside you and a stick-out handle?'

'Real isn't how you are made,' said the Skin Horse. 'It's a thing that happens to you. When a child loves you for a long, long time, not just to play with, but REALLY loves you, then you become Real.'

'Does it hurt?' asked the Rabbit.

'Sometimes,' said the Skin Horse, for he was always truthful. 'When you are Real you don't mind being hurt.'

'Does it happen all at once, like being wound up,' he asked, 'or bit by bit?'

'It doesn't happen all at once,' said the Skin Horse, 'You become. It takes a long time. That's why it doesn't often happen to people who break easily, or have sharp edges, or who have to be carefully kept. Generally, by the time you are

---

* Excerpt from The Velveteen Rabbit, by Margery Williams, New York: Avon, 1975, itals. author.

Real, most of your hair has been loved off, and your eyes drop out and you get loose in the joints and very shabby. But those things don't matter at all, *because once you are Real you can't be ugly, except to people who don't understand.*'

CONFERENCE XIII

'Blessed are the peacemakers.'

Matthew 5:9

ATTENTIVENESS TO OTHERS[1]

We spoke briefly of the essence of attentiveness to others in the last conference: to know revealed the true face, the face of Christ indwelling, which is being formed within, through a welcoming and loving gaze. A gaze that comes from the depths of a heart anchored in Christ by simple and habitual prayer.

Meanwhile, all of us have such bad egotistical habits and affectations to unlearn in this area, that it is perhaps not entirely useless to suggest some practical ways to help us cultivate a more profound attentiveness to others. It has to be said that this doesn't just happen spontaneously; in fact, one encounters it quite rarely.

The commandment of Christ is to love our neighbour; we are far from this, and in order to draw nearer we must learn. Let us begin humbly at the beginning.

To accept that others are precisely other. To rejoice that they are. To approach others in trust, with the faith that they are worth the effort, that there is something valuable, something beautiful and true in them. Experience shows that this is invariably true. 'The substance of love of neighbour is attentiveness. It is an attentive regard in which the soul empties itself of itself in order to receive in itself the being that it regards, just as it is, in all its truth' (S. Weil).

To be concerned for others for their own sake, not only in that tiny part of them which touches on my world, that is to say, in so far as the other is part of my world.

By nature, the psychological world of each person is gathered around their own self. Everything is seen from this angle. By grace, everything ought to become centred around Christ but even then, on Christ indwelling the self, so that it is still from the interior of self that everything else is seen.

In order to understand others we have to enter their universe, to know how to see with their eyes, feel with their feelings, to be them through coinherence and sympathy. For this purpose we must forsake our prejudices, our personal preferences, our stereotypes, our territory. All of these things make our attention selective, filtering our perceptions of others and reducing them, finally, to our own image.

To relinquish all anxiety for self-affirmation, all curiosity and criticism.

To be pure attention, not favouring any aspect, rejecting nothing, judging nothing – this is pure receptivity and under-standing.

To be conscious that each person possesses a fragmentary and limited version of the truth, from a particular perspective. The other always bears a valuable new clarifying insight. To pay attention to what the other says without partiality. Some-times the simplest see most clearly.

But the most important communication between people takes place at the infra-verbal level. It is direct communication from self to self, from heart to heart, from unconscious to unconscious, that is not conveyed by words, that is able to say the opposite from what is conveyed through words.

Know how to listen at this profound level. We shall become aware of a resonance in ourselves, in our heart, in our con-sciousness, of what is sounding in the heart and consciousness of the other. A resonance of sympathy and communion, or a negative, a defensive resonance in an area where our sense of personal security falters, when we have erected barriers that forbid entry.

In order to receive the truth of the other, we must let fall defences that prevent intimacy; we must know how to live the truth of ourselves.

The capacity to welcome the other is a function of the

capacity of our heart; the capacity hollowed out by life, by suffering, and above all, by love.

But attention to the psychological me of the other, to what the person is in the particular moment, is not enough – because the other is more than this. The other is, first of all, a person, a being capable of limitless understanding and love, *capax Dei* (having a capacity for God). The other is someone freely called to be and to love in the image of God, a reality in process of becoming. The truth of the person is this person God has created as he wishes them to be in this particular moment. Frequently we are unaware of the truth of the self, we hide it, reject it. And yet it is there, buried perhaps, but revealing its presence by ephemeral signs.

To pay attention, to speak to a divine embryo in the other, this is to take seriously its deep truth, it is to help it unfold, sometimes to reveal it to itself. Often the other will open up in proportion to our faith and hope. If our love is truly the love of Christ in us, it will find in the other the image of God that they are called to be. Our attentiveness is able to reflect to them their unrecognized divinity.

ATTENTIVENESS TO SELF

It is very clear that this subject of attentiveness is too vast to be treated adequately, as an aside, in these conferences on the Beatitudes. This is, above all, true in regard to attentiveness to self and to God. It is better to leave these subjects for independent development and to complete these conferences on the Beatitudes.

For the moment it is enough to say that attentiveness to self is not narcissism, blissful complacency in our selves, but a courageous and clear regard of our motivations and who we are; a way of being in touch with this unique being that each is called to become in Christ. The place of this birth, the depth of the heart, opens out into this divine being, is its image; it is in this image, become transparent, that God is known.

ATTENTIVENESS TO GOD

Attentiveness to the deepest self leads one beyond self: the image seeks the Archetype. Attentiveness to self and attentiveness to God are like two interdependent and complementary movements, the breathing of our deepest being: Lord Jesus (attentiveness to God) – have mercy on me, a sinner (attentiveness to self).

Prayer is entering into the depths of the heart and dwelling there in peace, listening that is receptive and responsive to this mystery of faith that is realized in the union of the heart with Christ. Attentiveness to God is the work of faith and love; its fruit is the union of love and knowledge to which it gives birth. God is not an object towards which we look. Neither is he merely the 'I' become transparent to itself, in which the knowing subject and the object are one entity. God is other than all of this, and he can only be known in his own light. Attentiveness to God is rather to be receptive to this divine light, which shines in the face of Christ and shines by grace in our hearts, than an activity of the intellect. It is above all poverty, faith, receptive emptiness, nakedness and freedom. It is eyes that are open in the dark, the desire of love. If God illumines the attentive heart with his light of peace, the shadows are not thereby dispelled – God is pure and ineffable mystery and it is as a mystery that he gives himself – but these shadows become luminous: absence reveals itself as transcendent Presence, the creation shows itself in all of its autonomous reality and complete otherness and yet as a sacrament of God of whom Christ is the human face. In this knowledge, it is not the subject that becomes transparent to itself, but the known Object that enfolds the knowing subject in its own understanding of self by means of a loving embrace. The Father begets us as children in his Word by the Spirit.

'Those who do the work of peace will be called the children of God.' The work of peace orders everything in us according to the order of love; it renders us completely receptive and attentive to that which is in truth; it opens us, finally, to the transforming light of God and enables us to enter the divine life. 'See what great love the Father has given us, that we should be called children of God and that is what we are' (1 John 3:1a).

Children share the same nature as their father. Here is the mystery hidden in the depth of our hearts, the birth of Christ in us.

> His divine power has given us everything needed for life and godliness, through the knowledge of him who called us by his own glory and goodness. These he has given us, through these things, his precious and very great promises, so that through them you may escape from the corruption that is in the world because of lust, and may become participants of the divine nature. (2 Peter 1:3–4)

– In Christ Jesus. 'And because you are children, God has sent the Spirit of his Son into our hearts, crying, "Abba! Father!" ' (Galatians 4:6).

'Blessed are those who are persecuted for righteousness' sake, for theirs is the kingdom of heaven.'

Matthew 5:10

The beatitude of the persecuted differs so significantly from the preceding beatitudes that it doesn't seem to belong to the early tradition. It alludes to the situation of the apostolic Church rather than the hearers of Christ. The reward of which it speaks (v.12) looks to the future and pertains to the persecuted, not simply because they are persecuted, but because they suffer on account of Christ; at stake is the reward for their virtue.

In the first beatitudes, the privilege of the disinherited attaches itself to their distress as such; because of it, God, in his royal generosity, owes it to himself to be their defender and to put an end to their suffering by effectively ushering in his kingdom in the Christ. The kingdom of God is near, already the poor are able to rejoice, their misery has come to an end.

However, the beatitude of the persecuted, if its formulation actually reflects the post-Easter situation of the Church, is nothing more than an expansion of a theme present in the preaching of Jesus himself: the decisive, eschatological importance of the decision of faith for Jesus, and the decision to take his side in his struggle against the powers of evil in the world.

Behind the constant fact of persecution of those who follow Christ stands the mystery of ancient warfare against the powers of evil by God and his servants. This struggle pervades all history, and it is more alive than ever in our day. In how many countries do we find people persecuted, imprisoned, murdered 'for justice', that is to say, for religion, integrity, the good? Christ is in agony until the end of the world, says Paschal.

> But rejoice insofar as you are sharing Christ's sufferings, so that you may also be glad and shout for joy when his glory is revealed. If you are reviled for the name of Christ, you are blessed, because the spirit of glory, which is the Spirit of God, is resting on you. (1 Peter 4:13–14)

We cannot be indifferent to the suffering of the members of our Body. We ought to assume them in our prayer, and they should put our minor personal suffering in perspective. We can understand in this beatitude all the suffering that comes to us in the cause of Christ. For example, people sometimes suffer in a hidden but profound way, because of their effort to live in fidelity to the light and love of Christ in them, an effort which demands ways of seeing and acting that challenge the mindset of those around them and are not understood.

In all of these cases, the duty of the Christian is clear. With eyes for Christ alone, we must not be disheartened (Hebrews 11:1—12:3). Nothing can separate us from the love of Christ (Romans 8:35), and from the same love, we ought to love and pray for those who, voluntarily or involuntarily, are the cause of his suffering. It means, perhaps, a long struggle, in tears, in prayers and humility, before love is the only radiance in our hearts, and before we know that it is to that love that the Spirit of Christ calls us. And let us be happy: the kingdom of heaven will be ours.

1. See Statutes 25. 13 and 33. 4.

CONFERENCE XIV

The poor: the kingdom of heaven is theirs.
The gentle: they will inherit the earth.
Those who weep; they will be comforted.
Those who hunger and thirst: they will be satisfied.
The merciful: they will be shown mercy.
The pure hearts: they will see God.
The peacemakers: they will be called children of God.
The persecuted: the kingdom of heaven is theirs.
– Your reward is great in heaven –

To end these conferences on the Beatitudes, let us meditate briefly on the promised blessedness.

It seems certain that all of the different expressions used point towards the same fundamental reality, and that this reality is most frequently described in the gospel as the kingdom of heaven. Land (promised), consolation, fulfilment, mercy (at the judgement), vision of God, to be children of God – all these are but various images of the kingdom. These images are linked to the messianic promise of the prophets, above all, Isaiah.

The primary text is Isaiah 61:1–3, a prophecy that Jesus applies to himself (Luke 4:18–19) and Matthew 11:4–5.

> The spirit of the Lord is upon me,
> because the Lord has anointed me.
> He has sent me to bring good news to the oppressed
> [*anawim*],
> to bind up the brokenhearted,
> to proclaim liberty to the captives,
> and release to the prisoners;
> to proclaim the year of the Lord's favor,
> and the day of vengeance of our God;

to comfort all who mourn . . .
to give them a garland instead of ashes,
oil of gladness instead of mourning,
the mantle of praise instead of a faint spirit.

The message of consolation is addressed to all sorts of suffering people. Isaiah 61 refers to the poor and afflicted, while the mention of those who hunger and thirst can be found among the oracles of consolation, of which Isaiah 49 is an example.

Thus says the Lord, the Redeemer of Israel and his Holy
One . . .
In a time of favor I have answered you,
on a day of salvation I have helped you . . .
saying to the prisoners, 'Come out,'
to those who are in darkness, 'Show yourselves' . . .
they shall not hunger or thirst,
neither scorching wind nor sun shall strike them down,
for he who has pity on them will lead them,
and by springs of living water will guide them . . .
break forth, O mountains, into singing!
For the Lord has comforted his people,
and will have compassion on his suffering ones.

(Isaiah 49:7–10,13)*

In this way, the Beatitudes appear as the proclamation of divine intervention announced by the prophets. Jesus presents himself as the Messiah (the anointed one) by whom God ushers in his ultimate reign of justice and peace for humanity.

How beautiful upon the mountains
are the feet of the messenger who announces peace,
who brings good news,

---

* See also Isaiah 55:1–3; 65:13; 66:10; Luke 14:15; Luke 13:29 (the eschatalogical banquet), etc.

who announces salvation,
who says to Zion, 'Your God reigns.'

(Isaiah 52:7)*

The reign of God, the ancient dream of the prophets, the hope beyond despair of the poor. God himself will intervene to put an end to injustice and suffering in the world. The prophets, and Orientals in general, attributed to God the role of a great king,† who was obliged to conduct his rule for the sake of the poor and disinherited, to take them into his care, not for any cause or merit on their part, but by reason of the demands of his own royal justice, conceived in this way.

The coming in question is the eschatological coming of God, at the end of time, for the last judgement of humanity. It is in this sense that Christ speaks in his discourse. His message is that in his person the reign of God is near, is even among us; the hour of decision, but also of salvation has arrived. The hour of salvation for the poor has struck. Not, however, in the sense of material consolation for their poverty. They remain poor, in terms of the goods of this world; but they will enjoy it because they know the kingdom of God is theirs and that they will benefit at the time of his advent. Their consolation in the full material sense will come to pass only at the Parousia, or within an individual perspective in heaven after death.

But the reign of God is not confined purely and simply to the last days. The kingdom already knows concrete existence on earth. To refer it to heaven by-passes the essential mystery and the scandal of the incarnation, of the voluntary poverty of Love in Christ.

The ministry of Jesus constitutes the beginning of the advent of the kingdom. It's not important that it bears so little resemblance to what the Jews were awaiting from the manifestation of divine royalty; it's not important that it remains so paradoxical –

---

* Cf. also Isaiah 40:9.

† It could equally be said that the role of an earthly king was conceived as a delegated participation in the royalty of God, and therefore modelled on it.

indeed, scandalous – for us, also, in the cross, in the all-too-human shortcomings of the Church, in the persistence, even, perhaps, the increasing presence of evil, of injustice and suffering on earth. What matters is that God in sending Jesus to the world has begun the process that will end in the glorious coming of his reign, and that Jesus, in sending the Holy Spirit from the Father, has introduced into history the divine energy of Love which now, secretly, already realizes and will fully realize the reign of God.

The human face of the Spirit is the Church and the sacraments, the word and active works of charity; it is all that there is of love and truth in the world, even when it itself ignores its deep source and its name.

The poor have already been given an earnest of their inheritance: the secret riches of the grace of Christ, his joy, his gentleness, his strength, and – above all – his love in their hearts. The living centre of their heart is mysteriously illumined and transfigured by the divine light that makes them children, co-heirs in the Son, inheritors of God, already sharing in the fullness of life and love of the divine nature. Everything is changed from within, everything is illuminated by the living light of hope in faith and charity.

They will be satisfied, they will receive mercy, they will see God, they will be called the children of God. God himself in Christ has guaranteed it.

'For this reason they are before the throne of God,
and worship him day and night within his temple,
and the one who is seated on the throne will shelter them.
They will hunger no more, and thirst no more;
the sun will not strike them, nor any scorching heat;
for the Lamb at the center of the throne will be their
   shepherd,
and he will guide them to springs of the water of life,
and God will wipe away every tear from their eyes.'

(Revelation 7:15–17)

It is tempting to analyse this beatitude, to talk about it . . . I would rather invite you to make contact with it in the depths of your heart so that it can be lived in truth. Like the Virgin Mary, guard all these things in your heart (Luke 2), hold in faith and hope this truth that is greater than your heart.

> 'What no eye has seen, nor ear heard,
> nor the human heart conceived,
> what God has prepared for those who love him' . . .

(1 Corinthians 2:9)

CONFERENCE XV

HARMONY

A life becomes harmonious when all of the elements that make it up work together towards the same end. They are reconciled one to another, and each has adapted to a common vision and goal. A harmonious life is a beautiful life, as a song is beautiful when the cluster of sounds of which it is composed blend together in a way that is pleasing to the ear, and are perfectly adapted to the feeling that it is trying to express.

To realize this harmony, all the sounds must blend together agreeably, and the most humble sounds have their importance and merit our attention.

Today, I would like to consider the place of the body in our contemplative life. The body is an essential dimension – I don't mean a detachable fragment – of the human person, and, if we want our life to come to its proper beauty, we cannot neglect it. If our bodily behaviour isn't in harmony with our life of prayer and quest for God, it becomes an instrument out of tune, which, over time, enervates our spiritual striving.

Interior beauty tends to form the body in its image in reciprocity, if it isn't hindered. At the same time, it isn't a question of the beauty of a physically perfect body but rather an interior light that shines through and transfigures even an ugly physique. Happily, we have all encountered such people. This is true human beauty.

Let us be clear. What we are aiming at shouldn't be the centre of attention in the spiritual life. We must not substitute a cult of the body for the contemptuous and somewhat brutal attitude of certain more or less dualistic spiritualities of the past. These at least had the merit of giving priority to high spiritual values. But this ought to have been done without crushing the physical aspect of the person.

Rather than embark on theoretical considerations, let us see how, in practice, we can harmonize our physical bearing with our spiritual seeking. It is a matter of consciously cultivating a physical deportment that helps the interior life, that facilitates self-discipline, recollection, profound attentiveness to self, to the other and to God. In short, that helps us live more deeply and harmoniously, to integrate all the levels of our human reality.

The monastic tradition has always paid a good deal of attention to the body's gestures. Fasts, vigils, postures for prayer, liturgy, bodily penance, desert wastes, exterior silence, the habit – all these things aim at helping our body to collaborate in our spiritual quest. We profit from them in the measure that we consciously take on this discipline.

The rhythm of modern life is so feverish, agitated and clamorous that the majority of people have to re-educate themselves in order to recover a rhythm that is in harmony with a deepening interior life. Stillness, silence, peace have to be learnt.

It's a question of something very generalized, an approach that pervades all our actions. It's difficult to characterize. It comes almost naturally where there is a profound interior life; but the reverse is true: to cultivate it enhances this life.

In order to live from the depths of the self we must learn to enter into it and remain there. In order to make our activity transparent to the inner light, we must make it serene and ordered. We must come to bodily mastery, not by striving that is angry, anxious, violent, but as one would engage a young, slightly impetuous friend, who needs a certain ascesis so that he will give a proper value to the best of himself. Gentleness, persistence, patience, a little each day, are the words that effect this order.

The work of gentling can only be done in peace. This peace is, above all, interior. It is based on our faith and our confidence in the love of God for us, on our being utterly at the disposal of his will, on welcoming all that he allows to happen to us, on love for every human being and every creature in Christ.

We seek to remove obstacles that hinder the flow of divine grace in our heart energy, of which we are carriers through the

Holy Spirit. It is appropriate to have an attitude of vigilant listening to the reality that we are, an attitude of responsive attentiveness.

There are psycho-physical techniques that can help this effort towards harmonization – yoga, for example. None the less, I would discourage you from putting too great an emphasis on yoga techniques (as with true Hatha yoga). First, because these techniques depend on the supervision of an experienced master and the context of a living tradition; otherwise they risk being hurtful, even to health. Secondly, because these techniques are conceived in the light of an understanding of the human person and a spiritual ideal that are different from those of Christianity. Their goal is an interiority closed in on itself, an en-stasis, whereas Christianity is a religion of love that results in an open interiority, an ex-stasis. This is to speak too simplistically of a great tradition, but it is enough to help us realize that the fundamental orientation is different.

At the same time, it seems to me that we can derive great benefit from certain elementary techniques,* the type of yoga used to master, stretch and calm the psycho-physical organism.† What seems to me chiefly necessary in our time for many young people is a certain training in psycho-physical stillness and in the mental concentration so necessary for the life of prayer. It is very humble work, if you like, that seeks to facilitate from a distance, both the active and passive aspects of the theological virtues, faith, hope and charity.

---

* Allotting a certain time each day (a half-hour is enough) to devote to vigorous exercise (gymnastic, or strenuous manual labour) is strongly recommended in order to maintain fitness and good health, and to reduce the risk of too much concentration on more 'contemplative' exercises.

† The majority of exercises presented in popular books of a 'gymnastic' yoga fall into this category, for example, D. Dunne, *Yoga for All*. The same is true of the series of exercises that Father Déchanet gives in *Christian Yoga*, but the overly enthusiastic and somewhat naïve approach of this author is not recommended, especially for beginners. He gives yoga much too prominent a place than is appropriate in the life of a Christian monk, at least in my opinion.

Below you will find some exercises; one or another might be useful, depending on what each one needs. *Moderate* use of this form of exercise helps maintain equilibrium. They are by no means obligatory. If you don't need them, so much the better!

ASCESIS

In our frenetic and stressful age, what follows seems to be a valuable aspect of asceticism: a cultivated stillness (*quies-hesychia*), a discipline of peace and silence in which a person may recover the ability to slow down for prayer and contemplation; also the ability to be present and attentive to others.

A smiling, natural, peaceful equilibrium.
Joyous renunciation of the superfluous, solidarity with the
   poor.
To follow the naked Christ.
Humility and purity of heart.
Entrance into the heart to find the kingdom.
Awaiting with all our being the coming of the Lord.
God is.
God is Love.
To be Love in Christ.
Prayer, charity, joy.

PHYSICAL EXERCISES

The goal of physical exercise is a certain refining of the body that facilitates its collaboration with the more sensible parts of the soul. Let us not seek a merely physical benefit. Regular practice is an ascesis that educates the will.

A. PRELIMINARY CONDITIONS FOR MAXIMUM BENEFIT FROM EXERCISE

- To be able to be totally and calmly focused on what one is doing, solely attentive to the present moment
- Purification of the memory
- Habitual discipline of the thoughts of the heart, of the eyes, of the imagination
- Confidence in the love of God and abandonment to his Providence:
    - –accepting everything that the body suffers (sickness, loss of mobility, death)
    - –accepting oneself honestly, not glossing even our most secret thoughts
- An attitude of love, of compassion, of welcoming towards all the creatures of God:
    - –calmness and equanimity in regard to self and others
    - –detachment and non-attachment to detachment itself
    - –a sense of non-possession, even towards the small-est thing
    - –treating the body with kindness
        to establish a dialogue with it
        to treat it as something alive and not as a machine
        to draw on its strength

B. ELEMENTARY EXERCISES

Seated exercises
These should always be done on a small stool or a cushion

the spine should be straight
the neck very relaxed (extremely difficult)
eyelids *always* closed
without rigidity

Standing exercises
> support should come from the base of the spine, not from the feet
>
> relaxation of each muscle, the 'knots'
>
> relaxation: undoing the knots in order to establish a golden thread
>
> energy should flow smoothly

I. BREATHING EXERCISES

Inhale as if you were inhaling through the top of your head (the parietal seams form a mouth), make the exhalation descend the length of the vertebrae *very slowly*, with closed eyes. In the emptiness, focus between your eyebrows.

Be aware of your respiration, which little by little should slow down – *prolong the exhalation.*

The most important exercise
This benefits circulation, elicits interiorization and relaxation. Stand with eyes closed, palms together, the tips of the fingers upward level with the chin or the lips. The feet should be a little apart, equidistant (raise the arms if necessary for balance: there should be a sense of balance, order, equilibrium). Raise one leg, knee forward, leg bent. The knee should be at the height of the navel, the foot should hang. Stand balancing on one leg only for several minutes. Repeat with the other leg.

When this exercise becomes routine, you will no longer have to think of body, leg, foot . . . but will be able to centre directly in emptiness between the eyebrows.

This exercise moderates respiration and promotes calm and stillness. It is important to do it with the eyes shut.

II. INTERIORIZING EXERCISES

Sit, eyes closed, very relaxed.
– focus between the eyebrows

– focus in the middle of the solar plexus
– focus in the heart
This exercise helps relax stiff muscles.
It enhances mental balance.
It should be done very slowly.

III. EXERCISES FOR SELF-CONTROL

Control of the voice
Be aware of the situations that cause you to raise your voice.
Most often this happens because of slight irritation with someone – this irritation may very well not concern the person you
are speaking to.

Custody of the eyes
(to be practised even when alone, but without rigidity or
exaggeration)
Control your curiosity concerning the things around you.
The more you are focused interiorly, the more you will have a
  sense of others and their signals.
Sustained practice of this exercise becomes a part of consciousness, a help to suspending all judgement, and all inappropri-
  ate movement.

Disciplined movements
Use only the energy required. Deliberate gestures, quietness,
  care with objects.
Good will towards and respect for every living being.

IV. RELAXATION EXERCISES

Standing: relaxation movement
Stand with feet slightly apart, aware, feeling yourself oscillating,
and allow your body to go with this movement, which describes
a nearly imperceptible circle. (If you're tired, this exercise can
be done seated.) Support for the body should not come from
the feet but from the base of the spine.

Seated
Become aware of your body, particularly the back of your neck,
your hands, your feet; relax them as much as possible – con-
firm your state of relaxation. Eyelids closed for these exercises.

In the beginning:
  a – Imagine, be a flower in bud, watch it open very slowly,
      absorb and become light. Internalize, transform yourself
      into light. (This exercise is suitable for beginners,
      because *all authentic exercise should be done free from
      images.*)

  b – Picture the sun surrounded by clouds
      little by little makes the clouds disappear
      see the sun outside of you, then inside
      then within the heart
      breathing should slow down little by little

Relaxation of the eyes: Palming
In darkness, the eyes find rest.
  Put the long fingers of one hand over those of the other in
the centre of your forehead, palms fitting exactly over the eye
socket, not allowing any light in. The hollows of the hands
permit the eyes to blink freely and don't press on the eyeballs.
In this warm darkness, muscular tension quickly drains away
and circulation improves. Do this exercise quite frequently, for
two minutes. It is more effective when accompanied by mental
relaxation and after 'swings'.

General release of tension: Elephant swings
Stand, head straight ahead, arms swinging, fingers hanging
freely. Put your feet flat on the floor, parallel, 25 cm. apart.
Slowly shift the weight of the body from one leg to the other,
turning your head and shoulders a quarter turn and allowing
the heel of the non-weight-bearing foot to leave the floor. The
weight-bearing foot simply pivots on its sole, the supporting
leg remains straight while following the rotation of the body.
During the fluid execution of these movements, the head and
neck follow, shoulders and arms swing by gravity. Count: 1 to

start, 1, 2, 3 quarter turn to the left, 4, 5, return facing front, 6, 7 quarter turn to the right, 8, 9 return to facing forward. Do this exercise as if it were a dance, something enjoyable. Inhale on 1, 2; exhale on 3–4, etc.

Little by little, the eyes don't note objects, vertebrae become flexible, internal organs return to their normal position. Neck, shoulders, chest are completely passive. When the view of the room seems to slip past it's a sign that the eyes are completely relaxed.

Fifty times in the evening gives tranquil sleep.

Fifty times in the morning refreshes after a bad night.

V. COMPLETE SEQUENCE IN A MINUTE

Salutation to the sun (preferably done in the morning)
Stand, body straight, feet together, hands in front of the chest fingers stretched, eyes focused forward, face relaxed.

Exhale.
1. Raise your hands above your head, stretching as high as possible. *Inhale.*
2. Separate your hands, turning the palms to the front; *while exhaling*, bend the body slowly, without bending the knees. Put your hands on the ground on each side of your feet, touching your knees with your forehead.
3. Supporting yourself with your hands, bend your knees and stretch your left leg behind you, head up. *New inhalation* during which the right leg is placed in the same position.
4. Without moving the position of your hands and feet, push on your extended arms so that your feet are as flat as possible. *Hold your breath.*
5. Always without moving your hands and feet, *exhaling*, lower your face and chest towards the ground, bending your arms. The knees should not touch the ground. The weight of the body is on the arms and toes.
6. Return to the position with the chest supported by straight arms while *inhaling*. Push your chest forward, face turned

up, but with the chin against the neck; make sure your legs are straight.

7. Pushing once more on your arms, make your feet as flat as possible again, body back, head between your arms. Hold your breath.

8. Bend the left leg and bring the left foot back between your hands. *Begin to exhale.*

9. Do the same thing with the right leg and foot. *Exhale completely.*

10. Raise the body, arms above the head. Inhale. Exhale deeply, returning your joined hands in front of your chest. Make two or three profound exhalations, and then repeat five times.

NB It is very important to coordinate the breathing as indicated. When the sequence has been learnt, each Salutation requires about a minute, when it has its proper rhythm.

Benefits: Exercises the whole body – muscles, circulation, controlled respiration, stimulation of internal organs.

Notes on the
Carthusian Order

The next volume in this series concerns vocation and discernment, and contains a detailed account of the origins and development of the Carthusian Order. However, a few notes to
accompany this first volume might be helpful.

The Carthusians trace their origins to the eleventh century,
the century of hermits and their experiments, the Cistercian
reform and the appearance of the Camaldolese. As with so
many of these experiments, the existence of an Order was never
intended by the man the Carthusians look to as their founder.

Bruno was born in Cologne around 1028, a precocious scho-
lar, but a churchman and an administrator rather than a creative
thinker like his contemporary, Anselm. By 1043 he was student
at Rheims and, in rapid succession, assistant professor, and
canon of the cathedral chapter. By 1056, he was Rector
and Principal of the cathedral schools.

A dispute with the corrupt archbishop Manasseh, loss of
office, possessions, and forced exile were catalyst for his
vocation. After Manasseh's deposition, Bruno was an obvious
choice for archbishop, but, renouncing everything, he began
his eremitical life at Sèche-Fontaine with two companions, followed, after four years, by the foundation in the mountains of
the Chartreuse, near Grenoble, accompanied by three other
clerics and two converse brothers.

Because of the crisis in which the pope of that time, Urban
II, found himself, and at his request, Bruno left the Chartreuse
and followed him in exile to Calabria. There Bruno founded
Sainte Marie de la Tour, but it is the Chartreuse that has
endured for over 900 years as the 'mother and source of our
Carthusian life'.[1]

It was only forty-three years (1084–1127) after the foundation of the Chartreuse by Bruno that Guigo, the fifth Prior, set down in writing the customs of the life that was being led there; and this on the insistence of other foundations that wanted to follow the same mode of life, and not because there was a need to codify the observance. Guigo's Customs are not the underlying theory of Carthusian life; they simply record the way of life of the first Carthusians. It's a matter of practical wisdom about spiritual and mystical ends. For the rest, Guigo returns us to the monastic tradition.

We are inheritors of a living tradition, handed on from one to another across the centuries, incarnated in the reality of the lives of monks who lived in these same places, generation after generation. They were motivated by the same faith, they sought the same God, they prayed with the same words, chanted the same melodies, without doubt, suffered the same trials. The last link is the generation that has preceded us. We see in them the bearers of the tradition of our fathers.

This immediate contact is very important. The transmission of a tradition is not accomplished only by the transmission of doctrines and practices. It is also done, perhaps in the first place, by a kind of symbiosis. It is a life that is transmitted, and the breast that nourishes the younger members of a community on its substance is the concrete milieu of this living community . . .

The motto *numquam reformata* (never reformed) that we display with such insistence doesn't imply a written law that has never changed from its inception. Rather, what we see is a living organism that adapts itself to changing circumstances, interior and exterior . . .

The Customs of Guigo were conceived for a small group of men. The three centuries that ensued saw the birth and expansion of a great Order. By the sixteenth century there were 195 houses [in the seventeenth century 555 were professed at the Chartreuse with 94.6% perseverance]. And what social and religious upheavals between the twelfth and twentieth centuries!: the Black Death, the great schism, the Protestant Reformation, the Counter-Reformation, the French Revolution, the suppression of the Order and the diaspora of monks, the return and renaissance of the Order in 1817; then a second expulsion and exile in Italy, the First World War, the return in 1940, the Second World War, Vatican II, the present world crisis.

This fidelity was not maintained by a mechanical repetition of what had gone before. It was a creative fidelity. It was a question of a spiritual reality, the search for God in solitude and in brotherhood, and each generation had to recover for itself the spirit of the vocation. Each generation has to live this adventure according to the truth (for us, as people of the twentieth century) and with a constant and ever deeper return to the sources, drawing on St Bruno, Guigo, the Chartreuse in the primitive freshness of its vision and in its saints across the centuries. A return to the sources also in the great monastic tradition, Western and Eastern. Above all, from a profound encounter with the Word of God in holy scripture. Our life is no more than a response to this created Word. It is in our being 'guided by the Gospel' that we go to the Father.*

It is perhaps this single-hearted, biblically based goal of Carthusian life, its balance of rigour and tenderness, its distillation of the radical message of the gospel and insistence on God Alone, and the austerity that enables the plunge into the abyss of Love, that contain the secret of its endurance.

'What do you seek?' This is the first word that Jesus speaks in the Gospel of John. It is the first question that Christ addresses to those who want to follow him.

The Prior asks the candidate who is to receive the habit, 'What do you seek?' We know the word of St Bernard, '*Ad quid venisti?*' It is a question we should continue to ask throughout our lives.

---

* Extracts from *The Way of Silent Love: Vocation.*

The Statutes are very clear. When a candidate presents himself to become a monk, he is asked about his motives and intentions. There is one criterion: that he truly seeks God alone.[2] How? In dying with Christ in order to live with him.[3]

Every other consideration becomes secondary, birth, social background, intelligence, etc., all that concerns the candidate's person; or for that matter, intention: the opportunity to study, human development, health, a search for exotic experiences, dissatisfaction with the modern world or the Church as it is, misanthropy, natural taste for solitude, renunciation, peace, and even prayer.

Over the long term only the search for God is able to give meaning to our life and create a balanced person. It is because they are, consciously or unconsciously, seeking something else that dissatisfied people who seem to have failed to reach psychological or affective integration are to be found in monasteries. Frequently they are engaging in displacement behaviour in some slightly marginal activity: studies, a responsibility, the 'reform' of the house or the order, etc.

Practically speaking, Carthusian life constitutes a unique integration of solitude and community. There are three sorts of monks in a Carthusian Charterhouse: choir, converse and donate, and all are dedicated to solitude. The choir monks are bound most completely to it in their cells (separate hermitages), meeting daily only for Matins and Lauds between about 12.15 a.m. and 2.30, conventual Mass, and Vespers. Once a week there is a walk in common, and on Sundays and greater feasts, refectory and recreation in common. The choir monks do manual work in their cells, along with *lectio divina*, reading, writing, and other occupations that help to focus a life of unceasing prayer.

The converse brothers and donates work alone as far as that is possible. They live in a symbiotic relationship with the choir monks; each is dependent on the other. They have more latitude in the Office they say, and in their choice of participation in choir, but their striving for union with God in love, interior solitude and unceasing prayer is no less rigorous.

The centuries-old tradition of fasting is kept, along with other austerities, not for tradition's sake but because of the immutable laws that govern the relationship between body, mind and spirit that the Order has distilled over the centuries from monastic wisdom, East and West. As the present volume has shown, within the Order there is an acute awareness of the uniqueness of each person's path to God, but, while mercy prevails, the monks are ever on the alert for appeals to 'modernity' that simply mask sloth or an immaturity that demands immediate gratification.

Knowledge of God can be communicated only by God to a person living in peace and waiting on God; it is impossible to transmit by human means beyond the 'contagion' of the Spirit, in which the fire of love is kindled from one life to another, although within the Charterhouse, modern contributions to human knowledge are not, of course, ignored. Carthusians are ordinary human beings with the same desires and failings as other human beings. One does not have to be a superman to be a Carthusian.

What is different about the Carthusians is that they are ordinary people who have fed the hunger that cries out in every human heart with the food of the gospel taken at its deepest level, for this food is Love, Love incarnate, crucified and risen; Love in whom sacrifice and priest are indistinguishable, and 'the monk likewise becomes both a priest and a sacrifice whose fragrance is pleasing to God,' and through this he 'shares the unsearchable riches of his Heart'.[4]

> The Christian is not a separate species of human being, but what each person is called to be. And the monk is not a separate species of Christian. He tries to be what each Christian ought to be. Conformity to Christ in faith, hope and love, this is holiness, and each person is called to this holiness.

'But what is it that I love when I love God?'* exclaimed
St Augustine. Like Augustine, the person who is drawn has
great difficulty in saying. Perhaps it is just this that is an
element of the attraction, 'deep calls to deep' (Psalm 42:7).
The time-lag between the reality of attraction that the beginners experience and the expression that they are able to give
it is notorious and sometimes poses delicate problems of
discernment. But it is certain that for a vocation to solitude
and prayer there must be a profound sense of God, of
his infinite mystery in which the solitary disappears by the
unknown paths of the desert. We can get to the unknown
only by unknown paths. God alone can lead to God. 'Alone'
– this little word weighs on the monk (*monos*) like an unbear-
able doom and a promise without limit that demands a
complete integration of his being in love and truth. This
solitude has meaning, exists in truth only as the expression
and the means to satisfy a thirst for intimate communion
which is itself a response to the enticement of love. Lovers
seek solitude in order to discover each other and become
one. Love alone suffices. Only Love suffices.

This is the great secret. All the hard language of stripping
is only the negative aspect of the language of love. For the
one who loves focuses all their heart on the beloved and
this does not require continual efforts of the will. *Amor
meus, pondus meum*, said St Augustine. Love, by the gravity
of attraction, inclines all our being towards the beloved. It
is in this way that the burden of Christ is light, because the
love of God has been poured into our hearts through
the Holy Spirit (Romans 5:5). As we become absorbed in
disengaging ourselves from our chains, one by one, let us
focus our attention and our heart on the Lord, asking him
unceasingly for the gift of love. The rest will follow, by the
grace of God.

> 'Let us burn with divine love
> we have become sacrifice.'

---

* Conferences Book 10, 6.

1. Statutes 4.31.1
2. Statutes 1.8.6
3. Statutes 1.8.7
4. Statutes 1.3.8

FOR FURTHER INFORMATION:

St Hugh's Charterhouse
Parkminster, Partridge Green
Horsham, Sussex RH13 8EB

Charterhouse of the Transfiguration
Arlington, Vermont
05250 USA

O Bonitas!